Beauty Before Comfort

Beauty Before Comfort

A MEMOIR

Allison Glock

ALFRED A. KNOPF NEW YORK 2003

THIS IS A BORZOI BOOK PUBLISHED BY ALFRED A. KNOPF

COPYRIGHT © 2003 BY ALLISON GLOCK

OWING TO LIMITATIONS OF SPACE, ACKNOWLEDGMENTS FOR
PERMISSION TO REPRINT PREVIOUSLY PUBLISHED MATERIAL
MAY BE FOUND AT THE END OF THE BOOK.

SOME NAMES HAVE BEEN CHANGED TO PROTECT ANONYMITY.

LIBRARY OF CONGRESS CATALOGING-IN-PUBLICATION DATA
GLOCK, ALLISON.
BEAUTY BEFORE COMFORT : A MEMOIR / BY ALLISON GLOCK.—
IST ED.
P. CM.
ISBN 0-375-40121-0
1. BLAIR, ANEITA JEAN. 2. GLOCK, ALLISON—FAMILY. 3. BLAIR
FAMILY. 4. NEWELL (W. VA.)—BIOGRAPHY. 5. NEWELL (W. VA.)—
SOCIAL LIFE AND CUSTOMS—20TH CENTURY. 6. CERAMICS
FACTORIES—WEST VIRGINIA—NEWELL—HISTORY—20TH CENTURY.
7. COMPANY TOWNS—WEST VIRGINIA—HANCOCK COUNTY—
CASE STUDIES. I. TITLE.

F249.N49 G57 2003
975.4'12—DC21
[B]   2002030184

MANUFACTURED IN THE UNITED STATES OF AMERICA
FIRST EDITION

For Dixie Jean and Matilda Mercy Law

There's something about the pottery. You build up quite a companionship, a comradeship, whatever you call it. You take a little bit of clay and mix it up with water and fire it and make something out of it—there's romance in that. It just gets in your blood.

—ED CARSON, POTTER, 1985

No potter that ever lived can be overlooked, no ware, however humble, can be despised.

—SATURDAY REVIEW, 1879

*All photographs from the personal
collection of Aneita Jean Blair*

Everyone has a story to tell. This is the story of my grandmother as she chooses to remember it.

Beauty Before Comfort

Anita Jean Blair

Bless her heart.
   That's what we say. It's a catchall.
"Aunt Sue's getting divorced."
Bless her heart.
"Velma lost her job at the bank."
Bless her heart.
"Crystal backed over the cat with her Cadillac."
Bless her heart. Bless the cat's heart.

And so that is what we say when we are told, "Your grandmother is getting worse."

Bless her heart, we say, although really her heart has never been better. The problem is, as always, in her head.

CHARLOTTE, NORTH CAROLINA, 2000

The tiny nursing home bedroom is crowded with family. It is my grandmother's eightieth birthday and we are trying to get her dressed. Though old, my grandmother is an able woman, so that is not the problem. The problem is style. We are dressing her for a party, her party, and so she wishes to appear festive, and the beige sweater, slacks, and boots her three daughters have selected for her are not cutting it.

"I don't think that will do at all," she says, tossing the sweater off the bed. "And no one is wearing those anymore," she says, squinting and pointing a crumpled arthritic finger at the ankle boots.

She is right, of course. No one wears ankle boots anymore, but her insistence on looking in vogue draws eye rolls and heavy sighs from her girls.

"How about a nice skirt and sweater set?" she suggests. "Something in a yellow, *my* yellow." Dutifully, her oldest daughter leaves to go fetch a new ensemble from the mall. Grandmother relaxes and leans back onto her bed. She eyes the group gathered around her, her daughters and their children and various boyfriends, girlfriends, husbands, and wives, and wrinkles her forehead.

"Where's Glen?"

Glen is her second daughter Jody's husband, an ex–pro football player prone to complaining.

"He's at the doctor's office," says Jody. "Something's wrong with his private area."

"Bless his heart," says Grandmother.

"He has bad balls," says Jill, her youngest daughter, cutting right to it.

"Well." Grandmother laughs. "That's the saddest story I've heard all day." And then: "Don't you all have anything better to do today than sit around staring at me? Stay any longer and I'm going to start charging rent."

•

Let it be said that there is nothing on God's green earth my grandmother would consider better than an opportunity to stare at her. She has spent at least seventy of her eighty-two years cultivating stares and making damn sure she has warranted the attention. To gaze at my grandmother is not a passive exercise. She's no Vermeer. She gives you bang for your buck—be it by making faces, cracking jokes, offering a peek at her undies, or any other shtick she can whip up for your amusement. She's beyond a pro. To look at my grandmother is to be made to feel special. It's an actress's trick, but my grandmother was never an actress, just the daughter of a factory worker born and raised in hillbilly West Virginia ("West-by-God-Virginia," she calls it), the proverbial coal miner's daughter, minus the coal and the redemptive sparkly career in Nashville.

"I was born depressed," she often says, only half-joking. Depression isn't exactly rare these days in West-by-God-Virginia, as a quick drive through Grandmother's old neighborhood confirms. Nearly everyone you see is overweight, stuffed full of triple burgers and seasoned fries, living on junk because junk is cheaper than a head of lettuce in most of West Virginia, and when you make shit money at the factory or the mine, you stretch your dollar as much as you can. Besides, a triple burger sure feels better in the belly than a head of lettuce, and most rural West Virginians take what comfort they can get.

Which is why they drink. And smoke. And sit very still on their porches, rickety slices of wood so worn, the nails snag your feet as you shuffle across. They sit very still in their folding chairs, the kind with the itchy plastic-fabric seat you buy at Wal-Mart for $1.99. They sit and they smoke and they pop beers with one hand, pushing down the tab with an index finger so the beer drains quicker from the hole and the cigarette butts drop in more easily once the beer is gone. They sit and wait until they forget what they're waiting for, and more often than not, they fall asleep in those itchy chairs, the plastic pressing into their doughy legs and arms like cookie cutters.

Sometimes they sing:

Oh, the West Virginia hills, the West Virginia hills,
Tho other scenes and other joys may come,
I can ne'er forget the love that now my bosom thrills,
Within my humble mountain home.

It wasn't always so bad as now, but West Virginia has never really had it good. It is a hard place, founded on hard land—"The only thing it's good for is to hold the world together," goes the joke—and the folks who live there don't expect any different. Those who do enter into a losing battle with Providence and go mad with the trying, as surely as rocks roll down the mountain.

"I ended up with my nerves," says Grandmother, describing how her home state shaped her. My grandmother's nerves are legendary, like Judy Garland's.

"Bring me a Xanax, would you, dear? Bring me a couple."

•

Time was, no one worked a room like my grandmother, Aneita Jean Blair. A slinky redhead with a knowing smile, she sailed through every doorway as if on a wave, ruffling each man and sending them sniffing after her like hounds in heat. In seconds, she would be surrounded. Drinks were brought to her. Cigarettes were lighted by a convoy of matches. She was fanned or draped with sweaters as the climate required. When she rose, all eyes stretched to watch her walk away, hypnotized by the tick-tock swing of her hips. My grandmother always found a reason to look back, and it filled her with a torrid joy to discover the men's eyes focused on places they shouldn't have been.

As a child, I lived with my grandmother now and again when my mother needed a break, which was often, being as she was in college and broke and rearing me alone in an attic apartment short on lightbulbs and food. A few hours' drive through the mountains brought me to my grandmother's house, a small white vinyl-sided two-story with a cement front porch big enough for a glider and a backyard big enough for a game of horseshoes, but not much else. I would run inside to see her, and she would grab my chin, tell me to stand up straight, then push me into the kitchen, where she'd prepared graham crackers and honey on a heavy white plate that felt cool when I licked up the crumbs.

"That's low-rent, little girl," she'd say as I tongued the plate.

"But I'm hungry," I'd whine.

"Fine to be hungry. Not fine to act like it."

I must have been around ten years old when I realized that my grandmother was not like other grandmothers. Men would call—plumbers, pastors, Boy Scouts—and she would work them into a lather. "Oh my! My robe seems to have fallen open. How embarrassing."

When the other town ladies dropped by the house in their elastic-waist pants and plastic shoes, my grandmother greeted them in suede go-go boots and a miniskirt.

"Great color on you, Dottie," she'd say as her neighbors stood speechless, eyeing her naked legs and chunky turquoise pendant, no doubt wondering why in heaven's name she'd bought *that*.

"I swanee," they'd cluck as they left the house.

"Bless their hearts," Grandmother would say as the screen door slammed.

Her golden years changed her little. Grandmother stayed chic. She did not wear her hair in a bun (she preferred to cut hers in the impish style of a French ingenue). She did not coo at babies. She did not dress in housecoats and slippers. She did not fatten up and sit in a rocker, patting her ample lap, and rasp in a warm, creaky voice, "Come up here and let Grandma read you a story." She did not, in fact, allow us to call her "Grandma" or "Granny" or anything as pedestrian as "Memaw." She permitted "Grandmother" and only that, and that is about where her grandmotherly qualities started and stopped. That's not entirely true. She baked.

She was an expert baker, and she swore that the day she used a box mix for a cake was the day they might as well put her away. She also baked pies, splicing the butter into the flour with two knives, instead of using a mixer. While she baked, my grandmother sang. Her voice was lilting and sweet, which nearly overcame the raunch of the lyrics, songs of her own creation, which inevitably referenced the scatological.

"Ah lasagne, piss on ya, shit on ya," she'd wail in full-on opera mode. I was young, but I was pretty certain that the other grandmothers I knew never sang phony arias about elimination while kneading pie dough.

No, my grandmother was different, had always been different, and, though she had paid dearly for it, had chosen to remain different, if one can choose those things.

Aneita Jean Blair was born and raised in Hancock County, West Virginia, same as me, until my mother found herself a decent fellow (from Kentucky), remarried, and moved us to North Florida, a dog's piss away from the Georgia border. (In predictable hillbilly fashion, my birth father flew the coop when I was a toddler, leaving my mother and me to scrap for ourselves.) Although Florida offered more amusement for a child—The beach! Orange trees! Alligators!—I preferred West Virginia, in no small part because my grandmother lived there and she was amusing enough for anyone.

I begged to go back, and my mother was happy to comply, shipping me off every summer until I was in high school and the lure of West Virginia gave way to other, more hormonal yens.

I remember the drive to West Virginia from the Pittsburgh airport, the impossible corkscrew of the roads and the dented iron railings that lined them. I remember how dense the leaves of August were, how dark it could look in the holler even at noon. I remember the metallic scent of land raped by industry and how it rattled your teeth. I remember bony dogs running free down the highway, clotheslines strung heavy with overalls, the sound of gravel under the tires, the cool of the air, the supple dapple of the light, and how my grandmother's voice rose and rang like a bell above it all as she sang on the drive home, the piercing white clarity of her song lending the whole worn scene a delicious flavor, a purpose.

"What'll I do with just a memory to tell my secrets to?" she'd sing as the road rumbled by. "What'll I do?"

Her voice sailed out the window, a stream of silk. *Ka-chump, ka-chump* went the road, and I would feel my body loosen with each mile, stretched open by her song and the exquisite melt of coming home.

As a child, West Virginia was my world. More specifically, Newell, West Virginia, a sad hump of a town paralyzed by poverty. I loved Newell with an inexplicable ferocity, the way a mother loves a screaming baby. "Country roads, take me home, to the place, I belong, West Virginia, mountain momma, take me home, country roads." It became a family joke.

"You want to go where?"

Well, I wanted to go anywhere my grandmother was, because my grandmother sang songs and made men blush and fed me graham crackers with honey and showed me how to walk in heels and how to braid my hair and how to be more than I thought I was in the world.

"Grandmother, my braid is uneven!"

"A man on a flying horse wouldn't see that."

From her, I learned how to tell when a cake is cooked, how to cock my head to appear interested in someone else even when I wasn't, how to make macramé plant holders, how to tell a joke, and, during one brash moment in a truck stop ladies' room, how to smoke gracefully.

"Exhale like you're bored. And look up. Always look up."

The first lesson she ever taught me was that dancing matters. Grandmother felt that a person, especially a gentleman, who did not dance was not a person with whom one wanted to spend much time. When she did come across men she fancied who didn't dance, she sent them away until they did. They always learned, because my grandmother was bitingly beautiful, and that is the second lesson she taught me—that beauty inspires, all of God's beauty, but especially hers.

I can still see my grandmother sitting at her dressing table, looking into the mirror. It wasn't much of a mirror, just a round fist-sized lens screwed atop a metal base painted to resemble gold. The base was wobbly, and to get an accurate reflection, she had to duck and bob around a crack in the lens. Still, it had the necessities: You could, with effort, still see yourself, there was a magnifying side (for plucking concerns), and it was portable, so should the house catch fire from some act of God, the mirror could be snatched up and carried to safety along with, should there be time, a handful of lipsticks and an eyeliner pencil. Children like myself, it was assumed, would fend for themselves.

Grandmother probably spent more hours in front of this mirror than she did the television. She didn't gaze into it willy-nilly, but she believed in presenting herself well, and that required a healthy time commitment. It required devotion. It required ritual.

Every morning, Grandmother would don her robe and sit at the dressing table, her makeup brushes laid out beside her like surgical instruments. She started with moisturizer, a thick yellow cream she applied generously from scalp to neck. Then she dabbed on concealer, under the eyes and around the nostrils. On top of that came liquid base to even out the skin. She shook the bottle as if making a martini and then smudged the pale beige goo down to her throat, taking care to prevent a tide line at the collar. Then she brushed on blush, a dusting on both cheeks and the nose. Then eye shadow, two shades, and eyeliner, one shade. Then mascara, top and bottom lashes. Then lip liner, around the edges and then coated over the entire lip. Then lipstick. Then blot, on a tissue. Then more lipstick. Then blot, on a second tissue. Then more lipstick. Then a once-over of loose powder to "set" the face. She finished with a self-administered pinch on each cheek for color.

This routine did not change for sixty years. The shades and the products stayed the same, and when fads like contouring and brow thickening happened along, my grandmother was not tempted. As a child in West Virginia, I watched my grandmother do her face almost every morning. I sat on the floor, silent, while she executed the same movements, brushed the same strokes, never skipping a day, never rushing through it, never, ever smudging lipstick on her teeth. To Grandmother, a woman who didn't bother to make the most of what God gave her was displaying a lack of fortitude. As far as she could tell, the only women who didn't make themselves up were lesbians and lunatics, and while she had nothing against either group, she certainly strove to differentiate herself.

"Beauty before comfort," she would say as she trimmed her brows and cinched her belts corset-tight. My grandmother is so beautiful that she has never once been comfortable, a cross she bears with the subtlety of Liberace. Even now, at the age of eighty-one, she has her hair colored weekly and doesn't descend the stairs without full makeup. If an opera spontaneously broke out at her nursing home, Grandmother would be appropriately dressed.

It is a legacy she has passed down to her own daughters, and they to theirs. Generations of women painting themselves to perfection, ramming their feet into tiny shoes, sucking in their bellies, dousing their hair with enough spray to gag a horse, girl after girl learning the value of being "as pretty as you can be."

As family legacies go, beauty before comfort is a particularly cumbersome inheritance. For my mother, it necessitates a minimum full hour of prep time every morning, time that lengthens as she grows older. For my youngest sister, it requires an arsenal of beauty products—enough to fill a second suitcase when she travels. For me, it meant coming to terms with the fact that in a long line of great beauties, I was not a great beauty, and that I'd better start honing my sense of humor.

For all of us, it means living with a low-grade anxiety, a murmur in our brains fueled by our collective self-consciousness and our compulsive sizing up of our place in any room—Who's prettier? Who am I prettier than?—as if our very survival depends on our ability to seduce.

For Grandmother, the pursuit of beauty meant something deeper. Born as she was in a factory town, tiny and blinkered and perched precariously on the banks of the Ohio River, beauty meant nothing less than freedom. Ugly girls didn't escape to Hollywood and sit by the pool in leather mules. Ugly girls didn't marry up and fly away on airplanes. Ugly girls got left behind and never knew any better.

Grandmother believed that there are people who tell stories and people who inspire the telling, and she intended to be the latter. "A pig's ass is pork," she would say when the local men pecked after her, wanting to know her heart's intentions. Or maybe, "It ain't lying if it's true." When the boys would confess their desires, daisies in trembling hand, Grandmother would smile and weave the flowers into a halo for her hair. Before it was all over, she would have seven marriage proposals and a body like Miss America and her share of the tragedies that befall small-town girls with bushels of suitors and bodies like Miss America, girls who dare to see past the dusty perimeters of their lives.

She keeps a memory book from this time, her youth, before she was tired and widowed and old, when she was cream-fresh and believed her life was as open as the road. All women kept scrapbooks back then, hoping somehow that their history would mean more than most. My grand-mother's is a three-ring brown plastic binder with black construction-paper pages holed out at the edges and snapped inside. The pages have worn through the years and many have Scotch tape bonded to the seams. In the book are newspaper clippings and birth announcements, ticket stubs and good-natured platitudes cribbed from local papers, bromides along the lines of "Though you have but little or a lot to give, all that God considers is how you live." (I can only figure she found these snippets ironic, as my grandmother has never shown the least bit of interest in God or any of his considerations.)

For the most part, there are photographs. Black-and-white images of her and her boyfriends, sitting on cars, standing on fences, the men smoking cigarettes in World War II uniforms, Grandmother fanning out her dresses to best advantage. On many of the shots of the men, there are love notes penned in the corners, hungry scrawlings declaring their affection for the girl behind the camera.

There must be more than one hundred of these pictures, I know because Grandmother and I have often looked at them. Every Christmas or Fourth of July, out comes the memory book and the stories.

"Now, that boy sent me a big bottle of Chanel Number Five from boot camp, I saved the bottle. And that boy took me to the Kentucky Derby; I had a mint julep. And that boy raised greenhouse roses. And that boy took me roller-skating. And that boy died in the war."

She tells me which boys she loved and which loved her. She tells me about her brothers and her sister and her mother and father. She tells me about her house and what went on there and how it was to be young in West Virginia, to be a skinny, eager child with disobedient hair and bottomless longing. Certain pictures are like songs, making her cry no matter how many times she sees them. Almost every snapshot is labeled neatly with the subject's name—including each photograph of my grandmother: "Aneita Jean Blair" tightly jotted in the white border at the top, a nod to the future she dreamed she'd have, one where strangers knowing who she was would matter.

917 Phoenix Ave Chester
Jean Blair Thornbury born here in
1920

CHAPTER TWO

The state of West Virginia was born in conflict and has
retained lo these many years a mulish attitude problem. The people born there are chippy. It's a birthright.

The state came to be in an act of war, when the western
half of the state broke off from its eastern parent, Virginia,
in 1863. The two sides disliked each other with familial
intensity. The western half envied the wealthy eastern half.
The eastern half was ashamed of the western half. The
westerners saw the easterners as idle slave owners. The
easterners saw the westerners as boorish rednecks.

"What real share insofar as the mind is concerned could

the peasantry of the west be supposed to take in the affairs of the state?" said easterner senator Benjamin Watkins Leigh on the floor of the 1829 Virginia legislature.

"Screw you," said the peasantry of the west.

Western Virginians were sick of the ridicule, of being overlooked when it came to building schools, of being dismissed as "woolcaps" by the richies who lived in the pampered south of the state. Then, around 1850, the state of Virginia borrowed $50 million for improvements and the construction of roads, canals, and railways. The only money spent in what would become West Virginia was $25,000 to build the "Lunatic Asylum West of the Allegheny."

It was not a promising precedent, and the two regions formally went at each other's throats. The rivalry played out in the legislature for years, until finally President Lincoln stepped in and pressured Congress to push Western Virginia's independence through. This decision "turns so much slave soil to free," he said. It was "a certain and irrevocable encroachment upon the cause of the rebellion."

Thus was born a state and the lasting tradition among its people of giving whomever they please the finger. "Mountaineers are always free," declares the state motto. This history was not lost on my grandmother.

•

Aneita Jean Blair was born at the foot of her mother's bed on September 30, 1920.

"I was born ugly," my grandmother says. This is a lie, but it is a lie she believes.

In the album, there is only one photograph of the infant Aneita Jean. It was taken on the Fourth of July and she is roosting on her father's knee, a lump in white cotton, with a black wick of hair falling down her forehead. Beside her, her two-year-old brother, Petey Dink, rests an American flag on his shoulder, his free arm raised to shield his eyes from the sun. A horse and buggy is parked behind them. It is impossible to tell if she was in fact ugly, but, given the gene pool, it seems unlikely.

On the day my grandmother entered the world, it was storming, and because her mother always kept the windows open, Aneita Jean Blair was not only ugly but in the rain. When her father rushed into the bedroom, Grandmother was already there, pinned down by her mother's foot, wailing and kicking in a runnel of wet. It is because of this that she says she is crazy.

"I'm crazy, you know," she'll tell you soon after you meet her. She is indiscreet. She tells the grocery clerk she's crazy, the bank teller, the librarian. She once met a boyfriend of mine, grabbed his arm, told him she was crazy, then suggested the two of them climb into a dog crate and "see what happens."

Aneita Jean weighed seven pounds at birth, a weight she would more or less carry until the first grade. She was a colicky baby, a crier. She spent the first years of her life in a foul mood, believing even then that a life without beauty is a pile of slop.

In a photo of her as a toddler, Aneita Jean is standing outside, her mouth screwed into a knot of agony, her hair sticking up like a pitched tent. When she was two, her older brother, Petey, had given her a doll that frowned, which made everyone laugh, but which she despised and pinched when no one was looking.

"Everybody thought it was funny," she says. "I didn't think it was so damn funny." And then: "Buster Keaton never smiled, either, and everybody was mad for him. Ah, horseshit feathers."

In public, Aneita Jean would stand eyes forward, lips flattened, hair chopped close to her neck, reeking of defiance and looking lifetimes older than the little girls next to her, with their eager smiles and shy eyes. Family lore has it that it would be a full three years before she ever smiled. Three years, never so much as revealing a tooth.

•

I'm going to leave here one day," she'd say to her mother years later, her head nestled in her lap.

"Why would you go and do a thing like that?"

"Because."

It wasn't much of an answer, but then, as a little girl, she hadn't really thought it out. It was an instinct. She was going to leave, become a painter or a singer; she was going to wear dresses with sequins and make art and meet dark men in suits who smoked pipes and nodded their heads in approval.

"No one leaves here, Jeannie," her mother, Edna, would chide, tucking a curl of hair behind her daughter's ear. Edna herself had moved only twice, arriving at the new spot within a few hours of the last.

That few people escaped West Virginia was true, but an irrelevancy to Aneita Jean. Ugly or not, she decided that by the time she was sixteen, she'd find a man who would carry her over the mountains to a place where all the women lolled about, resplendent in chiffon and diamonds, and all the men looked like Errol Flynn before he started drinking so much. Someplace glamorous. Like Pittsburgh.

CHAPTER THREE

I couldn't stand the dirt. The alleys. The ignorance. You
know how you drive through towns and wonder, Why
would anyone live here? That's how I felt. But we lived
there. We lived there our whole dingdong lives."

Aneita Jean Blair was the second child born to Edna
Virginia McHenry Blair and Andrew Charles Blair. Edna

was a natural flirt. She was Irish, bosomy, and spirited, with jowly cheeks that vibrated when she laughed. Andrew, a Scotsman, was not a jovial person and seemed in a constant state of mystification as to how he'd ended up married to one.

The year my grandmother was born, West Virginia was in the throes of a moonshining epidemic. Every month, more forbidden stills were discovered, and in a raid just weeks before Aneita Jean's birth, state officials found a still in a nearby church, news that sent Edna into hysterical laughter. Andrew didn't cotton to irony, so a month later, when the Ceramic Theater showed *The Family Honor,* "a picture that sharply contrasts right thinking and right living with false pride and evil deeds," Andrew Blair made sure his wife saw the show.

Andrew and Edna would have five kids altogether, all spaced roughly two years apart. The first was Andrew junior, whom everyone called Petey Dink, then Aneita Jean, then Forbes, followed by Alan, and, finally, Nancy. The Blairs were an attractive family, but Petey Dink and Aneita Jean were dealt the best genetic hand. Both were tall and lean, with wide eyes that jumped off their pale round faces. Both had small plump mouths, and with their translucent skin and golden red hair, they looked every inch like their Celtic forebears.

Forbes was a blonder, blander version of Petey, more like his father, sturdy and tense, while Alan and Nancy were born with brown curls and longer faces. They looked like mournful cherubs, and they studied intently while Petey and Aneita Jean robbed apple orchards, their laughter trailing behind them like a kite.

They all lived in a brown brick and clapboard Victorian at the corner of 917 Phoenix Avenue, in Chester, West Virginia, just on the cusp of the good neighborhood, where the people didn't have to stretch sugar or send their kids to the government depot for cans. Just a few blocks away, they could wade into the woods and play amid the dogwoods, rhododendron, wild violets, and long, wispy trees that rustled like bamboo.

Their town was known for two things—pottery factories and not being as pitiable as its downriver neighbor, Newell.

Pity being a relative thing in West Virginia, the distinction boiled down to small details. Newellies still kept chickens in their yards. In Chester, there were fewer chickens and more flower beds, and on occasion, in the nicer homes, wallpaper.

The Blairs had flower beds and hand-sewn curtains cut from heavy cotton bark cloth printed with tropical leaves. They had a porch and a walled yard and a stairwell up the center of the house. There were four bedrooms and one bath. The street out front was gray brick, and in either direction there was a view of the factory smokestacks.

Like Newell, Chester was a blip on the east bank of the Ohio River, part of a cluster of small towns that make up the panhandle, Hancock County, a region of steel and brick, but mostly clay. The clay was unique. Plentiful and unusually malleable, it was perfect for making crocks, jugs, stoneware, and china.

Potters lived there, whole generations of them, growing up in cramped company houses, knowing only the job they were trained to do and the folks around them. Starting as early as 1830, people moved to what is now Hancock County, discovered the clay, became potters, and stayed. It was a marriage of resource and craftsman, and it was a marriage for life. "The second-oldest profession," they called it.

The clay along the Ohio River had a blue tint and smelled of standing water. Once in your nose, the scent never left, just dug deeper into your pores, so each breath reminded you where you were. It was persistent in other ways, digging into fabrics and under fingernails, like white blood, thick and seeping, growing crusty when it dried. Most potters didn't even bother trying to eradicate the clay; there was always more carried in their pant cuffs, in their hair, on their toothbrushes. Andrew Blair was a potter. And when his sons grew old enough, they, too, served their time in the factories, until the war called them away to more epic fates.

Throughout Aneita Jean's life, the Blair family was well known in the valley. The family's combined good looks and social acumen made them easy to spot. Forbes was an usher at the theater. Petey Dink danced with all the ladies, and danced so well that even the wives among them never refused. The whole family, save Edna, was dapper, but even she transcended her plain frocks aided by her round biscuit cheeks and knowing black eyes. Her husband favored layers of starch, stiff shirts and vests and jackets, so crisp and pointy, he looked to be cut out of cardboard.

In one family picture, Petey, fifteen, wears a floral-print necktie with a rumpled dress shirt and high-waisted pants. Aneita Jean, thirteen, wears a pleated skirt and wide-collared shirt. Forbie, eleven, aping his father, looks strangely adult in a herringbone suit, while Alan, nine, and Nancy, seven, sport fitted sweaters and stovepipe pants. Together, they seem to sing from the page, the clothes incidental trappings rustling around their collective confidence; except Alan.

Alan Blair had the misfortune of being born agreeable in a family of severe stoics and manic charmers. He was neither the oldest boy nor the youngest child. He was not the handsomest or the smartest or the cruelest. He was not a jock, a scholar, or a delinquent. He was just good old Alan Mead, shy and curly-headed, and he kept low to the ground and quiet. (Later, he would become an elementary school science teacher who rarely mentioned how he had piloted a drone plane through the mushroom cloud of the first dummy atomic bomb test, or how, as a full commander in the war, he had nearly died in a hurricane off the coast of Japan when his plane pitched into the ocean like a javelin.)

His older brother Forbes Wesley was quiet, too. But his reticence was a manifestation of control and a touch of snobbery. His father, whom he closely resembled, told him that he was better than everybody else, and Forbie believed it. His haughty air won him few friends in the valley. He didn't mind. Such was the cost of superiority. In the future, his truculence would make him a significant force in the Republican party, friends with the likes of Hoover and Reagan.

Nancy, the youngest, was a change-of-life baby, born when Edna was in her forties. Aneita Jean thought Nancy's was the most beautiful face she'd ever seen. It was perfect, with skin as lively as water and hair darker than molasses, and she spent a lot of time pretending Nancy was her baby.

Petey Dink, the eldest child, was the most magnetic of all. Lean and beautiful as a greyhound, he was quick-witted and full of beans. He wasn't much for schoolwork, believing himself smart enough already. He preferred stealing—candy, comics, cigarettes. His teachers tried reprimanding him, but they found it impossible against the tide of his charm.

"I'm sure I could concentrate better if I wasn't so distracted," he'd say with a lewd grin when they confronted him about his failing grades.

An instinctive athlete, Pete mastered football and baseball, then quit sports, finding them less stimulating than the company of women, up to and including his sister, Aneita Jean, a girl he adored, even if she was a little loopy.

"He thought I was nuts," says Grandmother. "But he loved me to bits."

The Blair family resembled the others in Hancock County only in that they were large, Scottish, and struggling. "We were never going to be wealthy," says Grandmother. "But my father wanted us to have class."

And so Andrew dressed his children like adults, and stressed the value of self-improvement. He made rules forbidding most childhood games like tag and hide-and-seek. And he made rules for conduct. Manners were of the utmost importance, as was grammar. At the Blair house, you stood up straight or were poked in the spine with a stiff finger. If your jaw fell open when you read, it was soon smacked shut from the chin.

"Quit your crying," Andrew would say whenever his children washed up on his knee with troubles. "There's a price for being special. You want to be like everybody else?"

"He had a hard life," Grandmother says in a level voice. "His mother was run over by a train."

•

The Blair house sat on a corner lot, right at the Harker pottery trolley stop. Because of this, it was a social hub. As potters waited on the front porch for the trolley, Edna would feed them rich slabs of homemade chocolate cake, fan herself with her napkin, and chortle at the stories they shared about the pottery. She liked hearing about life beyond Phoenix Avenue, what men got up to behind closed doors. She could imagine them there, slapping one another on the back, hauling ware, biting into their apples around that big wooden plank they used as a lunch table. She hadn't been to the factory herself. Andrew wouldn't allow her to visit, so she rarely went farther than the porch.

"He wasn't jealous," my grandmother explains. "He just thought it looked bad. He found my mother disgraceful because of her weight. He used to take her picture off the mantel and slam it on the floor."

Still, Edna didn't want for attention. She had the potters, who never tired of her cake or her company, and who shook with laughter when, indecent or not, she matched them joke for joke. Edna tittered most of all. Aneita Jean would sit at her feet, watching her face crack, anxiously mimicking the pitch of her mother's laughter.

There are just a few photos of Edna in the memory book. In one, she is old as old gets, standing outside next to a neighbor, smiling in her apron, her hair pinned back in a tousled bun. In another, she is young, sitting beside a window in a ladder-back chair, her hands clasped behind her head in reverie. She is gazing off to the left, her face heavy, her eyes shaded with sadness. She wears a linen dress with lace draped along the collar and sleeves. Her hair is in the same loose bun.

Edna Blair mesmerized her elder daughter. Aneita Jean was in awe of her mother's size, the way her breasts rose like sacks of flour under her apron, how her rump jutted out like a shelf. She often stared at her mother's fleshy arms, which shook like hung laundry and were badly seared from the too-small oven. Big as Edna was, the men cared little. "Most men didn't want any bag of bones back then," says Grandmother. Besides, Edna had ripe skin and a bow mouth and the endearing idiosyncrasy of not knowing how sexy both were. And so when the men laughed, it was because she was funny, but also because in their hearts they imagined for that moment what it might be like to be wrapped inside those giant arms, buried into the soft folds of her chest.

Sometimes, on her way into the house, Edna would turn suddenly and make a garish face, her eyes yanked down to her cheeks, her lips bulged from underneath by her tongue. This would send the potters roaring. Aneita Jean watched her mother and learned without trying how easy it was to please a man. Food and laughter and willing eyes. Everything else blanched to nothingness with time. At least that is what she believed then, as a child cushioned in the shadow of her mother, cake crumbs on her chin, the sweet of it still packed in her teeth.

Aneita Jean knew of no other mothers who made faces. Nor any who made men laugh. The other mothers she knew were sour and tired and barely smiled at all. Sometimes, these women would talk about Edna Blair.

"Sure seems your mama has a lot of time on her hands. What does she get to all day?"

"Well, we know it's not housecleaning."

The truth was, Edna Blair was sick. Diabetes. The disease made her fat and blind and ambivalent to housework, neighborhood gossip, and rules of decorum. Aneita Jean tried to curry her mother's favor by cleaning feverishly. She scrubbed the floors and sills, scrubbed everything really, until you could lick it and taste nothing but wood. But Edna didn't care about dirt or stains or having floors clean enough to lick. She didn't mind much in fact, not rain, or owning only one dress, or a hole in a boot. She was content to lounge on the porch in her colossal wicker love seat, eating cake and sucking the icing off her fingers.

Edna told no one about her illness because she knew how pity hollowed a person out. She had felt it from her own mother, Mewey, who had unloaded her like bruised fruit on the first willing taker, love being a luxury someone as damaged as her unhealthy daughter couldn't afford.

Edna had been working as a court typist when she met her future husband. He was selling shoes. Mewey took one look at Andrew in his sharp wool suit and decided here was the man for her baby girl. Andrew married Edna because, sickly or not, she was beautiful, with loosely pinned hair that curled around her ears like ivy. Besides, dating was not his priority. Edna had other ideas, but she knew she could not disappoint her mother. It didn't matter that adoring Andrew Blair was about as easy as falling up a well.

"You're sick, girl. Who else is going to marry you?" Mewey said.

And so, married off, Edna headed upriver to join a new

class of people. She and Andrew were wed in Columbiana County on August 26, 1913. After the wedding, Edna did her best, but Andrew Blair was not one for pleasure. He was temperamental, moody, and prone to meanness. He was also exceptionally handsome—tall and svelte, with a thin nose, wide-set eyes, and blond hair, which he slicked back with vigor. He had a plump bee-stung mouth, which shamed him. As soon as he was able, he grew a mustache to cloak his lips, and any remaining trace of carnality. He shaved it once, and it made my grandmother cry, so shocking was it to see his beautiful lips.

The Blairs' first apartment was in Wheeling, West Virginia, a flat in a line of brick row houses, two stories high, with cement porches and shuttered windows. Each floor held one apartment, as did the basements. Because the interiors were cramped and dark, people kept outside as much as possible, congregating on the porches, legs swung over the ledges, or sitting shoulder-to-shoulder on the stoop. The tight quarters left no room for privacy, an irritation to Andrew, so the Blairs moved to Chester as soon as they could afford to.

There, people quickly learned that Andrew Blair was a stern whip of a man, a taciturn Scot purged of any inclination toward revelry by that train that had flattened his mother and knocked his father into a lifelong wall of silence. The only things that brought Andrew to life were music and his garden. He was known for growing the tallest peas in the valley and for his skits in the pottery minstrel shows, where, behind his blackened face and floured lips, he felt safe enough to sing, dance, and run his body hobnobby-wild across the stage.

•

There are two photographs that capture Andrew best. In the first, he is sitting cross-legged on a tree stump. The trees behind him are leafy with the outgrowth of late summer, their wilting shadows dense and far-reaching. Despite the season, Andrew is dressed in a long-sleeved dress shirt, cuffs ironed and buttoned. His trousers are wool, also with ironed cuffs. His boots are snugly laced to the ankles and his tie is knotted up around his throat. On his head rests a wool cap.

His hands are loosely folded in his lap, arranged like flowers. His face is stiff and marked by measured boredom. The net effect is prim sophistication, a look wildly out of place in the rural West Virginia summer heat, or in West Virginia at all, for that matter. Here is a man who has forgotten, or is trying his damnedest to forget, that he is perched atop a stump in the middle of a disregarded nowhere.

The second photo was taken in the fall. Andrew is again in formal attire, this time a wool suit. He has been photographed from the feet up as he lies prostrate atop a stone wall. It's a silly angle, one obviously contrived in the fun of an afternoon at the park, a horsing-around sort of snapshot, except that Andrew is not smiling. He has assumed the position of a goofy young man, but his face will not relent. It remains a tight mask of thinly veiled annoyance. The soles of his shoes appear to have been, God love him, scrubbed.

When Aneita Jean was born, her father held her at arm's length.

"Well," he said after a time. "She'll do."

It was Andrew who decided to name my grandmother Aneita Jean after his sister Jean, whom everybody called "Jean Jean the Beauty Queen." In retrospect, this may have been a mistake, but that did not stop Aneita Jean from later naming her own daughter Jody Jean, nor did it stop Jody and her sister Jennifer from naming their daughters Jean. Names are history, constant and resonant, and so what if the first Jean turned out to be a loon.

Jean Jean the Beauty Queen was married to Robert Woods, a navy captain of some note in Pittsburgh high society. She had a daughter, Dorothy Jean, seven years old, who had flashing green eyes and auburn ringlets that bounced beside her cheeks. They were an abundantly happy family, and so it was a full-on tragedy when Robert's fighter-bomber went down in the ocean, leaving them alone. They managed for a few months, but things were never quite square. Jean Jean took to her bed or to walking around the house, circling like a ghost, nodding her head to no one. Dorothy was left alone, and she, too, grew quiet. Then spring arrived. The sun shone hot and clear and Jean Jean decided she would drive her daughter to the beach in Maryland. There, they dug sand castles and played guess which hand has the button. Dorothy ran along the shore and Jean Jean chased her, scooping her up from behind, making Dorothy squeal. For lunch, they ate bologna sandwiches and oranges. Then, after a rest, Jean Jean the Beauty Queen took her daughter's hand and walked into the ocean.

"We're going to see Daddy," she said.

By all accounts, it was ponderous going, but she persisted. Dorothy Jean struggled and broke free, making it to shore and into the arms of bewildered strangers. Her mother kept on. Never looking back to her child, she pressed farther and farther into the sea, her body bobbing in and out of view like a buoyed cork. The last thing Dorothy Jean saw was a froth of white sliding over her mother's hair, as if she were removing a slip.

After the funeral, seven-year-old Dorothy was sent to live in Indiana with her uncle Rob and his wife, Mildred. No one mentioned her mother until a generation later, when time had made it safe to talk about.

"Crazy, she was," says my grandmother. "Like me."

Grandmother had met Uncle Rob and Aunt Mildred in Indianapolis the summer before she turned ten, a year before cousin Dorothy would move there.

"I'm not saying they were dull people, just that they were dull people," Grandmother joked.

Aneita Jean and her father drove the Nash Ambassador to Indiana. Not many people in Chester, West Virginia, had cars, and the Nash, a blue-and-orange beauty, wasn't driven all that much. Usually, it sat idle in the shed, a monument to Andrew Blair's hard work. The car was intended for special occasions, like the Fourth of July parade, or hauling ware to sell on the road. So when her father announced that the two of them would be taking the Nash to another state, Aneita Jean nearly fainted.

It was strangely humid the weekend the two of them set off for their visit. They were sweating before they left Phoenix Avenue.

"Daddy . . ."

"Too warm to talk, Jeannie," her father snapped, sitting tall as corn in his suit and tie, even though it was hot enough to make the pavement bubble.

They drove in silence. Aneita Jean wore a starchy dress, which clung to the backs of her knees. She tried to peek underneath to see if it was staining, but she didn't want her father to notice, so mostly she sat very still and counted farm silos. These were the safe years, the comfortable years between father and daughter. Before the girl starts looking too much like her mama and dragging boys home like baggage. Before the father sees her growth and feels his age and his helplessness and it roils in his stomach like a beehive. No, those times would come later, replete with whippings and restrictions and all the other futile gasps of a parent losing control of his child.

Rob and Mildred had just married, and the two wanted to celebrate with Andrew. On the drive, Aneita Jean imagined all sorts of revelry—fancy dinners and grown-ups sipping wine. As it turned out, Mildred and Rob were as festive as her father, and the celebration consisted of apple juice and chewy pork chops eaten at home.

Mildred barely talked, just a word here and there, followed by a dry sniff to show her disapproval. Upon meeting Aneita Jean, she sniffed quite a bit, first at her dress (which was sodden), then at her hair (curls steamed to the back of her neck), then at her manner (inquisitive), which she found inappropriate for a child. The sniffing was particularly effective, as Mildred's nose was as pointy as a pencil.

Anteater, thought Aneita Jean.

After dinner, they all took a walk around the neighborhood. The houses seemed so big to Aneita Jean, if only because you could see for miles in every direction. There were no hollers or cricks in Indiana. The world was smooth and endless.

As they strolled, Aneita Jean began to limp. Something

was hobbling her foot. She tried to hide her pain, but her father noticed.

"Stand up straight," he said.

"It's my foot, Daddy."

"Take off your shoes," he commanded. He examined her small pale feet and sighed. It was a seed wart, a kumquat-size growth on the arch. "Looks like we're going to the hospital."

Mildred began sniffing like a locomotive, but Andrew shot her a look and she stopped.

At the hospital, they scooped the wart out like ice cream. Aneita Jean held her father's hand and stared at Mildred's nose as the doctors worked, wondering if it would be possible to stick a grape on the end, and wondering if Mildred had ever tried.

When they left on Sunday, Mildred stayed inside the house while Rob waved good-bye from the stoop. Andrew waved back, a curt to-and-fro movement.

"Daddy?"

"Yes, Jeannie."

"I'm sorry."

Her father said nothing.

"I didn't mean to cause trouble."

"Too hot to talk, Aneita Jean." And so they didn't; they just sat still, staring ahead, the heat flattening their heads like dropped bricks.

CHAPTER FOUR

Blame the clay. As a 1879 history of Hancock County explains, "The traveler who journeys in the cars upon the Ohio shore or upon one of the numberless steamers that float upon our beautiful river will no doubt observe quite a number of huge piles of clay of a bluish gray color, that lies at the foot of the hills along the West Virginia shore. Such a settlement upon the Rhine in Germany or upon the Tyne in England would have a history of a thousand years or more, made interesting by a hundred legends of love and war; while here, fifty years will antedate all this industry and nineteen twentieths of all this population."

William Thompson built the first true pottery in West Virginia during the 1850s. The pottery sat three hundred yards below what would one day become the Newell Bridge. Thompson and his hires made yellow ware—thick, sturdy tableware colored yellow and striped with blue or cream. They used water from the hills and clay from the riverbed. The clay was clean and had a nice hand.

This was not news. A mile across the river in East Liverpool, Ohio, potteries had been operating since the 1840s. Entrepreneurs smelled opportunity in the clay and the river, no one more so than English-born James Bennet, who built the first regional pottery in 1839. More immigrants followed, mostly from Staffordshire. In no time, potteries dotted the river like moored barges, their beehive kiln chimneys squatting and sputtering smoke at regular intervals, as if they were giant towering pipes sucked from below.

A gold rush followed. Towns that were once described by visitors as "forlorn" became hot spots. "East Liverpool is full of clay and coal and contains about 700 inhabitants," wrote one potter in a 1849 letter home to England. "There are markets open to receive every cup of ware that is made. It is impossible for you to starve."

As industry grew, social programs lagged. In a rush to capitalize on the clay, schools and city services fell behind. In 1881, only 800 of the eligible 2,200 children attended school. The rest were working with their families in the potteries, where wages were $13.96 a week in 1887, two and a half times what the same potters earned in England

and about $4.00 more than other tradesmen. Children were essential to the success of a pottery. Making china is labor-intensive. Jigger crews, groups who took clay from its raw form to the mold, were often made up of three people from the same family, who were paid as a team. A child was a cheap way to get the light labor done without squandering a third of the take. In 1880, 12 percent of all pottery workers were women. Fifty-two percent were children, half of them under age sixteen.

As railroad expansion continued along the Ohio River, materials and additional labor became easier to import. China lines expanded and potteries converted to more mass production. By 1900, East Liverpool, Ohio, was known as "America's Crockery City," and the population of the valley swelled tenfold. From 1870 to 1910, the numbers grew from two thousand to twenty thousand in East Liverpool alone. Ninety percent of the population worked in the ceramics industry.

It was an unusual scenario. Nowhere else in the country did one trade so completely dominate the daily life of a community. The potteries provided more than jobs: They functioned as social hubs, sponsoring baseball teams, dances, picnics. They brought in circuses and parades and shows at the Ceramic Theater. Conversation was about potteries and pottery technology. The newspapers ran a daily column called "Pottery News," which included reports on accidents (fires usually), kiln repair, and the ever-threatening competition from the Far East.

Hardships were rarely mentioned. Potters liked their work and complained little, even though each position had its extreme drawbacks. A jiggerman threw clay onto a mold and pressed it into shape. He was assisted by a mold runner, who carried the pressed clay from point A to point B, and a finisher, often a woman or child, who rounded edges and sponged the faces of the clay for blemishes. A good jigger team produced about 2,760 plates a day, the mold runner walking about fifteen miles before his nine-hour shift ended, carrying over 34,000 pounds of clay.

The clay itself had to be bubble-free before use, and so workers had to be capable of lifting one hundred pounds of raw clay, which they would cut in half with brass wire and then smack together to force out the air. The clay started as tubes thick as watermelons and long as a man's torso. These sat like weeping tree stumps, two by two, on tables until the flattener snatched one up and smacked out the air, burping it into submission.

After pressing, a kiln placer would put the uncooked ware into protective containers, called "saggers," and then stack the saggers as high as eighteen feet in a kiln. Saggers were carried atop a kiln placer's head to make the process of loading the kiln faster. To keep the weight from crushing their skulls, they rolled up cloth and wore it headband-style, calling them "kilnman's doughnuts." After firing, kiln drawers emptied the saggers, spending their whole shift hoisting burning-hot ware from kilns, their hands wrapped only loosely with cheesecloth.

There were also cup turners, who added feet and pedestals to china, and casters, who made sugars, sauce-boats, and other types of hollowware. Mold makers did just that, peaking production at one hundred pieces, because if used beyond that, a plaster of Paris mold would have sucked up so much moisture from the clay that it would begin to dissolve. Handlers stuck handles on cups, brushers smoothed clay, and dippers glazed baked ware.

And then there were packers, coal haulers, and myriad specialty positions, all of which required strength and speed to make items that, once done, would shatter at the slightest impact.

As the years passed, a new generation of potters was born in the valley. Time didn't diminish the potteries' magnetism. Men from Virginia, Kentucky, Ohio, Pennsylvania, and even Tennessee continued to come, lean and grasping, riding the rails or hiking the banks of the Ohio River. They were coming to a place thick with fable. A place they'd heard about, like California.

Soon, mass production had replaced fine craftsmanship, and the newer, more efficient potteries subsumed the antiquated boutique potteries, which relied exclusively on manual labor. Crockery City was crowded. Across the river, Newell and Chester were becoming the brave new pottery worlds. Unlike East Liverpool, which had grown to its limits between the twin barriers of hillside and river, Chester and Newell offered fresh possibilities. They had the same clay. And in West Virginia, the hill slopes were largely empty, the riverbank land primed for habitation.

What was needed was a bridge. In 1897, the first bridge to connect East Liverpool with Chester was built. Streetcars ran over it, carrying developers to West Virginia and potters to Crockery City. In 1900, Taylor, Smith and Taylor opened a pottery in Chester. The Edwin Knowles and Harker Pottery Companies would follow them.

Not to be outdone, the Homer Laughlin China Company began construction on the Newell Bridge on June 2, 1904. It would cost $250,000, and was erected just a quarter of a mile from the Chester Bridge. It opened a year later, on July 4, with a celebratory first crossing. HLC bought acres of land in Newell. They also bought a pottery site large enough to house a thirty-six-kiln factory, what would be the largest pottery built to date.

Other potteries saw HLC as foolish; it was hubris to build so large a factory on the whiff of a promise. Barely anyone lived in Newell. Certainly not enough people to staff a thirty-six-kiln factory. But it was HLC that prospered, while its competitors, hobbled by inadequate factory designs and outdated equipment, began shutting down their kilns. The bridge and HLC's promise of steady work brought intense expansion to Newell and Chester. In 1906, only a few houses stood in Newell. By 1907, there were more than 130. HLC not only constructed the bridge and the plants but laid down streets, erected more houses, and created ball fields. HLC either built or bought everything in Newell, down to the streetcars, the waterworks, and the schools. In 1917, the company even produced a car, the Homer Laughlin, a stretch convertible sports car with stitched leather seats and gleaming running boards.

The Blairs settled in Hancock County the same year. Andrew became a potter as soon as he could and quickly rose through the factory ranks to become a decorator, the most sought-after position in the factories. Decorators, also known as hand painters and liners, didn't have to hoist crates or sweat over kilns, and they were the most highly paid clay shop workers. Andrew spent his days trimming plates, cups, bowls, platters, goblets, and gravy boats with liquid gold. He'd take a tiny brush, no thicker than a rose thorn, and hand-line the edges, one after another, precisely and neatly, allowing no margin for error. Liners had prestige, and a staff of decal girls, women who would add flowers and garlands to the plates and cups before firing.

The decorator's kiln was the smallest. It measured only six feet high and burned at a lower temperature, just hot enough to set the colors and decals, but not so hot that it cracked the glaze. Different colors required different temperatures, so pottery was loaded on shelves and separated by ceramic stilts. After firing, the ware would cool and kiln-men would draw the pieces out, now baked to a brilliant shine.

Andrew recognized his good fortune and worked tirelessly to preserve it, often logging double shifts for weeks at a time, never stopping even to read the newspaper. While he may have settled for a common wife, Andrew Blair refused to succumb to the conspiracy of circumstance that had brought them together. He pined for culture. He taught himself how to play the ukulele and the mandolin. Then he taught others, for a price. He shied away from what he saw as low-rent habits, such as gambling and public affection. He did spit tobacco, but only in private and into a tureen he'd painted with deer and hunters in jaunty red caps.

He was not one of those other people, the men who soaked their shirts through with sweat and had clay packed under their fingernails even on Sundays—sour-smelling men in ill-fitting pants, spitting as they laughed. Andrew knew he was different. He never wore anything that didn't fit, never left the house looking less than altogether dandy, his trousers cutting a sharp line down his thigh, his coats free of pottery dust. When he trimmed his prize peonies, he donned a tie. He walked ramrod-straight, and he valued vertical posture in others. It bothered him to no end that his wife was stooped, burdened by her diabetes and her immense weight. Lazy, he thought.

When he wasn't at the pottery, he was in his backyard studio, making china dogs with gold eyelashes or bunnies with silver bows to sell on his own. Blairware, he called it. He had a hand-cranked wheel, a circle of marble that sat on top of a cast-iron stand. It was on this wheel that he spun plates painted with gurgling babies, ballerinas with lace skirts, and mewing kitty cats, their claws tipped with purple dye. He stamped "A. C. Blair" in liquid gold on the bottom of each frilly little plate and china novelty.

In time, he created other lines. Although Andrew Blair was not a member of the Ku Klux Klan, he liked their business, so he founded the A. C. Blair Klan Plate Company by snatching up blank plates from Harker and HLC and painting them with Klan motifs. The best-selling items were the platters that were painted red and yellow, with a fiery cross in the center, and those with a masked Klansman on horseback, the cross ablaze in the background. They are collector's items now, these plates. Prized by the same type of men who covet Nazi helmets and Civil War medical kits.

Hancock County was a hotbed for the KKK, especially during my grandmother's youth, when they focused their rage on the east end of the panhandle, where many of the area's black and Italian potters lived. The Klansmen operated under the dubious motive of enforcing blue laws, and they broke into homes, ostensibly searching for liquor. They also marched through the potteries, hooded and draped in white, demanding that the bosses fire any Italian workers. The police did little to stop them, as those who weren't intimidated by the Klan were generally members.

So strong was the Klan's influence that Chester became the first city to have a junior order of the KKK, a division that was created in 1923, when thirty-five boys were in-

ducted. The same year, they celebrated their perceived dom-
ination with a parade down the main streets, marching in
full costume in the shape of a cross. Twenty-five cars and
twenty thousand members attended.

As far as Andrew Blair was concerned, the angry men
who marched and assembled on the hill before their bon-
fires were good customers, polite to *him* anyway, and only
a fool would pass up an opportunity to make cash money.

To attract their attention, he'd have Aneita Jean sing
and dance in front of a card table he had set up. Any old
song, just sung loudly. It embarrassed her, but one didn't
say no to Andrew Blair, and so when he said, "Get up, girl,
and show these boys what you can do" at the rallies, or the
roadside, or the potters' picnic, little Aneita Jean gathered
herself and belted out whatever tune they'd practiced in
the car on the way there, wriggling and tapping as the men
laughed.

There is a photograph from this time. In it, Aneita Jean
and her father are sitting side by side, dressed in minstrel
costumes. Andrew is wearing a full mask and top hat, his
tattered overcoat draped with a flowing white shawl, tied in
a bow at the collar. Aneita Jean is in a similar torn coat and
loopy bow, but her face is painted black, with inch-thick
white pancake lining her eyes and mouth. She sits awkwardly, her right hand gripped at the fingertips by her
father, her left arm glued to her side by his embrace. Her
eyes look hollowed out, fearful. Her mouth hangs open
slightly, as if she were struggling to breathe.

Aneita Jean never liked the men at the Klan rallies. It
scared her not to see their faces. It made her uncomfortable
that they all seemed to know her daddy, and that he knew
them by their raspy voices. She would watch them circling

around on the hill, their crosses aflame, and snuggle closer to her father's chest.

"I want to leave, Daddy," she'd say softly, fearful they might overhear and come running back, robes flapping behind like hateful phantoms.

"Hush up, Jeannie."

In time, Blairware and the Klan plates became popular enough that Andrew strung a bell from his studio to the kitchen in the main house so that Edna could summon him once his meals were prepared. Only then would he stop painting and emerge into the light of day.

"We never ate out," Grandmother says. "The one time we got to go to the hamburg shack, Forbes got so excited, he threw up."

Andrew's fear of poverty and dedication to his work only made him harsher. My grandmother remembers the first time she saw him come undone. Her mother had asked her father to bring her some ice cream from the kitchen.

"Goddamn it, Edna," he snapped, "there's people in wheelchairs and they're getting their own ice cream. *People without any feet* getting their own ice cream."

The next day, he caught Edna hitching a ride home from Mr. O'Malley. She had gone to market and gotten tired while walking back to the house. When she got out of the car, Andrew spotted her. He waited until she was inside the house, then took a vase from the china cabinet and shattered it at her feet.

"Pick it up," he hissed. Aneita Jean rushed over and started piling the china, little pieces on top of the biggest, like she'd been taught.

"Not you," he said, his teeth tight. "Her."

Andrew waited until his wife started the slow, painful

process of bending over; then he turned around and stomped outside to his studio.

Free, Aneita Jean ran to Edna and threw her arms around her legs.

"I'll clean it up, Mom. You go and sit down."

"Oh, would you?" she answered, her face red as she struggled to stand up. "That would be fine."

Aneita Jean never saw her mother cry. But there were times when she heard her late at night, creaking in her rocker, the only sound the whine of wood on wood. She would creep down the stairs and watch her mother sway, eyes barely open, looking half-dead, like a lost dog on the highway. Like she'd been poisoned.

It was the same face her father wore when he came home from the pottery in a foul mood. Edna would leave the front porch and busy herself in the kitchen, preparing dinner, her face as blunt as all those other moms Aneita Jean knew, thick and still, as if there were marbles sunk in her cheeks. Aneita Jean noticed how the air in the house seemed to curdle with her father's presence and the suffocating weight of his expectations.

Now and then, Andrew would arrive home in good spirits. On those days, he would pick up his mandolin and play for the family. Aneita Jean and Petey Dink would dance, while Edna, Andrew, and Nancy clapped along. Forbie would sit in the corner, perturbed at the disruption.

The music echoed loudly in the house, trailing out the windows like vapor. Passersby would peek inside and see the Blairs dancing and singing like a sideshow act, and they'd think them the happiest lot on the block.

CHAPTER FIVE

How far he traveled the forest wild
No one can tell, no one knows;
But it's a sad, sad story
Of ages long, long ago.

Faint hearted, worn and helpless,
He came to a mountain stream;
And there amid the whispering pines,
He dreamed his last sweet dream. . . .

Upon a beechnut tree he'd carved,
"My name is Strange, and strange the ground;
Strange it is that I am lost
Never on earth to be found."

FROM "LEGEND OF STRANGE CREEK,
WEST VIRGINIA," AUTHOR UNKNOWN

There was beauty in Hancock County, to be sure. Hills of green and the twinkling Ohio River. Fields of wild-flowers hemmed in by hand-hewn fences. There were pockets of loveliness, and if you walked far enough or squinted tightly enough, you could see them and pretend they were bigger.

It was easier before the potteries came. In the first half of the nineteenth century, the valley was identified with apples, Willow Twig apples, which tasted vaguely of lime and flour and kept all season. It was their longevity that made them so desirable, and they became the chief commodity of the region, profiting the orchard owners, the pickers, and the hoopies who made the thousands of wooden barrels used for apple storage and shipping, sometimes as far south as New Orleans.

These were the magic days, before industry found West Virginia and set about tearing down its beauty and its peo-

ple. Before mines, mills, and potteries and the uniquely
West Virginian practice of removing whole mountaintops
to dig out coal and other resources, which were then
promptly shipped to enhance the lives of people living in
other states, where things like decapitating mountains were
prohibited. Once the clay got noticed, the apple business
quickly gave way to the more profitable and compact pursuit of china.

"Everyone went to work in the potteries," says Grandmother. "That was just what you did."

Making plates takes time, as long as fifteen days,
depending upon how many glazes a piece receives. Pottery
production starts in the slip house, travels to the mold
shop, the clay shop, the bisque kiln, then a holding ware-
house, then the dipping shed, the gloss kiln, the gloss ware-
house, and finally to the saggers, who box the whole kit up
and ship it to Woolworth or Sears, so housewives can buy
something sweet for their kitchens.

The potteries themselves are rugged work spaces,
cramped, airless warehouses stuffed chockablock with over-
sized vats and carts stocked high with output, the floors
made of chunks of wood laid down like bricks, soft enough
to prevent dropped china from shattering. Everywhere you
look, there are teetering masses of cups, bowls, and plates
rolling along dusty oil-stained floors damp with water and
littered with scrap clay curled up in the corners like sleeping
dogs. Pop bottles are stuck on the rafters, which are
scratched with graffiti—"I love this place," or "Ray Cobb,"
or sometimes just a heart with initials. Beside them, a sten-
ciled sign, ANYONE CAUGHT THROWING CLAY WILL BE SUB-
JECT TO IMMEDIATE DISCHARGE.

The kilns are basically giant ovens, large enough to

swallow a six-foot man walking upright, his head stacked with a dinner service for twelve. Down the center run railroad tracks that carry the carts holding the ware. Beside them are pyrometric cones made of heat-resistant plastic. When the coal or gas burns hot enough, the cones melt, signaling to the potters that the ware is baked.

Potteries are both dry from kiln heat and wet from the clay, and when you walk through the halls, you're hit with the changing climate, tiny punches of hot and cold air smacking against your skin. Metal ductwork hangs above like thrown spaghetti, random and clogged, looking as useless as it undoubtedly is. Woven above it is a similar chaos of wires, some of which drop down to hold bare bulbs caged in plastic. There are buzzing fluorescent lights, strings of pulleys and fist-thick chains, and everywhere, everywhere, worn wooden planks, split, dusty, and rounded from use. Most bow with the weight of idle china, while others are slung over crates for use as tables or shelves, or, come lunchtime, as benches for potters to straddle as they eat their mustard and cheese, their cotton aprons idle on their laps like napkins.

Pottery air has a dank sooty scent. When you inhale at a pottery, you suck in flint, minuscule particles of ground sand that float in the air and settle first in your nose, then in your throat, and then in your lungs. Too much flint in the lungs causes a disease called silicosis or "potter's asthma." In the thirties, they gave out masks to the workers most at risk, the shovel men, who loaded clay and kiln coal from trucks onto wheelbarrows. But working with a breathing mask was slow, and shovel men were paid by the hour, so few would wear them, preferring the future risk of a clotted lung to the more imminent threat of starvation.

There were other health concerns. To start, kiln smoke
kept air quality poor. So dire were risks for factory employees that as far back as 1863, the Children's Employment
Commission wrote a warning about "potters as a class,"
claiming that "both men and women represent a degener-
ated population, both physically and morally." The commission further claimed that potters were, "as a rule,
stunted in growth, ill shaped, and frequently ill formed
in the chest. They become prematurely old and are certainly short lived. They are phlegmatic and bloodless and
exhibit their debility of constitution by obstinate attacks of
dyspepsia and disorders of the liver and kidneys and by
rheumatism." Health inspectors in 1912 testified that of
thirty-seven potteries tested, only three were rated as
"excellent." The rest had "low ceilings, inadequate window space, crowded conditions, poor ventilation," and
many other failings, which made working there risky.

These reports dissuaded few workers and fewer factory
owners. They kept on potting and coped by drinking.
Drunkenness was so prevalent that in 1915 the Ohio Board
of Health theorized that, among other things, "the industrial inducement to alcoholism was chiefly in proportion to
the amount of dust inhaled."

Worse than the dust was lead poisoning, often suffered
by the women and children who hand-glazed or dipped the
china. Lead in the finish would enter the bloodstream
through the skin. It took the teeth first, turning them navy-
black, starting at the gum line, then seeping down until the
tooth jiggled out, the root dead from its toxic bath. Sometimes, the fingernails darkened, too, progressing from the
cuticle toward the tip, as if you'd bruised your finger and
bled under the nail. Soon enough, the lead would take resi-

dence in the bloodstream and line the arteries like bedrock. Once deposited, the victim experienced nerve damage, brain damage, cramps, vomiting, and an inability to eat. The more lead, the more irritability, clumsiness, paranoia, headaches, until, over time, the potter suffered irreversible retardation or a cumulative dementia that ended with either a coma or death.

Children were especially vulnerable, more often experiencing the "nervousness, insomnia, hallucinations, convulsions and sometimes frank psychosis" expected when lead had entered the bloodstream.

The poisoning was insidious because it started so slowly, with such vague symptoms, that most men and women had no idea they were killing themselves until they had passed the point of no return. In many pictures, they are smiling, gums black as a swamp, unaware of what awaits them.

In 1913, fifty-three pottery workers died from pottery-related illnesses: 37 percent from potter's asthma, 20 percent from lead poisoning, the rest most likely from fires. Still, despite all their drawbacks, potteries paid the bills, and so potters never spoke ill of them, much the way farmers never curse the weather. Hancock County wasn't the kind of place that tolerated complainers.

Instead, pride blossomed. Especially at Harker, Taylor, Knowles, and Homer Laughlin China. Unlike the other potteries that evolved from English roots, HLC was a tribute to local talent. (The Laughlins were so bonded with the pottery that long after they had moved to California, many members of the family still had their ashes sent back to the valley to be interred.) Even their stamp—the logo inked onto the bottom of every piece that left the factory—was a direct challenge to their English competition. It was an American Eagle disemboweling a Staffordshire Lion, with the name Laughlin scrolled beneath in soothing curlicues.

Every man my grandmother ever knew worked at one time or another in the potteries. Some would go on to the brickyard or the steel mill or the armed services, but all started their working lives in the heat of a kiln, pronounced "kill" by the people who manned them.

If you lived downriver, you were a hoopie, like Edna Blair. Hoopies were folks who made a living doing the bottom-dweller work, like cleaning out the cooper shed, which smelled worse than soured broccoli, or packing the barrels of pottery that were sent upriver and made by the folks lucky enough to have factory jobs. Even if you had one of those factory jobs, at the pottery or the rubber works or the sawmill, if you still lived downriver in Newell, you stayed a hoopie. Even if you'd never had to bend barrel iron, or smelled the cooper shed (which was unlikely), you stayed a hoopie, because you lived where the hoopies did and not upriver one mile, through the narrows, in Chester.

Hoopies got their name during the apple days. It was a nickname for the men who made their living bending iron hoops around shipping barrels. Over time, the label grew to include not just those who put staves on barrels but those who breathed the same air—spouses, neighbors, sympathizers, until finally it became synonymous with low class. It was both an insult and a point of pride to be called a hoopie. A hoopie was not someone you wanted your daughter to marry, but then, you didn't want her saddled up with anyone who believed himself better than a hoopie, either.

If you lived upriver but on Newell's border, you were a low-ender. Barely better than a hoopie, but better just the same. A quarter of a mile higher up, and you became an upper-ender and probably owned more than one tie. And then there were the hillbillies, backwoods families who shot and ate squirrel and whose kids wore no shoes at all. Hillbillies were considered superior only to the river squatters and the blacks.

The Blairs were low-enders. As such, they lived comfortably, although not well. Unlike Newell, where the houses were constructed cheek by jowl, with only a string of yard between them, Chester offered two strings of yard, enough for gardens and fountains and gazing balls, globes of colored glass that reflected the surrounding green. The Blairs' gazing ball was blue and sat in the center of the yard, offering a rounded view of the garden and the house. My grandmother remembers staring into it and thinking it looked like the smallest world she'd ever seen.

After HLC opened its Newell factory in 1907, a behemoth of a plant designed to employ twelve hundred workers, it took little time before virtually every resident of Chester and Newell worked locally, just blocks from their homes, walking the brick sidewalks or riding trolleys to the factories. Spurred by its success, HLC spent the twenties expanding. In 1914, it constructed another plant. In 1920, the company hired Albert Victor Bleininger, the foremost leader of ceramic engineering. Bleininger was a clay genius, and it was he who showed HLC how to use continuous firing tunnels.

Before Bleininger, pottery was fired in forty-foot-high brick kilns shaped like giant beehives. The kilns were hand-loaded with saggers full of unfired pottery. Workers would brick the kiln opening shut and light the coal. After the pottery fired, they had to wait for the kiln to cool, then remove the brick door before unloading the ware. With HLC's new tunnel kilns—long brick tombs open at each end and floored with railroad tracks—ware was fired continuously by the cartload. Each cart traveled down metal tracks at about fourteen inches per hour, baking in up to two-thousand-degree heat for about fifty-five hours. This sped up production so much that one kiln could now produce as many as 84,000 pieces daily, an amount that would have taken months to complete before.

With Bleininger's help, HLC built Plant Six, a gargantuan eight-hundred-foot-long building. Its construction required 6,000 cubic yards of concrete, 600,000 bricks for the walls, and 1 million feet of lumber. Around this time, HLC also unveiled their factory showroom, a decadent 50-by-150-foot space lined with gilded moldings and carved wood. Heavy leather chairs and couches were placed alongside walnut shelves decorated with pottery. The room was meant to befit the "dignity" of pottery and assert HLC's dominance of the industry.

"The splendor of medieval Venice!" proclaimed *The Pottery, Glass and Brass Salesman*. "A bower of delights," said the *East Liverpool Review*.

HLC seemed, like the economy, unstoppable. They made deals with Woolworth and Quaker Oats. Ads showed a woman's well-manicured hand pulling an HLC bowl from the cereal box. "Get china in each box of nourishing oats!"

By 1929, HLC employed the largest workforce it would ever have, 3,500 employees, prompting then manager W. E. Wells to dub the company "a giant among dishes." HLC was now the largest pottery manufacturer in the world, occupying sixty-seven acres and more than a mile of land along the riverbank. The company owned seven plants, six continuous ware kilns, three continuous decorating kilns, sixty-one periodic ware kilns, and thirty-eight periodic decorating kilns. To meet the demand for local housing, the pottery bosses and local backers erected rows of company homes in the vertiginous landscape, one butting up against another, with tiny napkin-size yards behind and small porches out front, where folks would sit and smoke, yelling to their neighbors sitting on their own porches, sitting and smoking. The roads were made quickly and carelessly of brick or, sometimes, strips of tar, cut like french fries and dumped in clumps on top of the dirt. The sidewalks were constructed from local bricks and buckled over tree roots. The streets were hardly photogenic. Just house upon house, their rafters rubbing, lining roads that all led to one place.

On one side of the factory sat an undulating range of hills tented by foliage, a bulwark of green pierced by obtruding rocks, many of which fell to earth in violent avalanches. This prompted the locals to erect signs warning WATCH FOR FALLING ROCKS, as if once you recognized you were beneath one, you could actually duck out of its furious path. On the other side, the Ohio River flowed by, cutting through a wall of golden gray rock, rippled and burned at the top like a meringue.

Just outside of the towns were woods. Dense and leafy hollers that dipped suddenly and rose again, like God's footprints, pooling leaves and deadwood in their gullies, catching forever the sweet smell of rot. There were streams and mountain springs popping out of nowhere like leaks. The few interior roads mirrored the sinuous coil of the hillside; high or low, there was only rock or green, towering tall and heavy, as the path you traveled twisted in on itself like a sleeping snake. Between the woods and the river, there was no room for the horizon, just the factories, perched thread-close to the water, flanked by smokestacks that emptied a steady flow of soot into the air, darkening the sky with their fleecy ink.

By the time my grandmother was a young girl, the HLC pottery bosses had become the undisputed rulers of the town. There was no mayor or police force. Emergencies were handled by neighboring counties with more traditional city infrastructures. The pottery bosses owned the schools, the electric company, the waterworks, the bridge, the trolley, the parks. They were all members of the Wells family, wealthy locals who, along with the Aaron family of Pittsburgh, purchased the pottery from Homer Laughlin in 1896. The Wellses lived, fittingly, at the top of Newell's biggest hill, propped against the edge, looking down on the town.

Like most tycoons of the era, the Wellses saw their patronage as a social duty. Together, they built and maintained public spaces, held parties, and did what they felt was right to help their small town prosper. They bought merry-go-rounds and hired trapeze artists to perform at the local parks. They lured radio personalities from Pittsburgh to appear at parades. They handed out Russell Stover candies for Halloween, and allowed the town children to frolic in the woods around their homes. Mostly, they lived lives that the townspeople could envy, traveling to Europe and Africa, playing tennis, entertaining celebrities, eating exotic meals, and having every moment dutifully recorded in the headlines of the *East Liverpool Review:*

WELLS FALLS IN FIRST CHAMPIONSHIP ROUND
IN GOLF TOURNEY!
300 POUNDS OF ROCK CRYSTAL SHIPPED FROM BRAZIL
FOR WELLS FIREPLACE!
WELLS, NEARLY KILLED, POPS JAGUAR IN GUATEMALA!

When W. E. Wells died in 1931, he was honored with a tribute from Proverbs: "The hand of the diligent shall bear rule. Seest thou a man diligent in business, he shall stand before kings."

The Wells family's compound sat on top of Newell's highest hill, overlooking the factory and the Ohio River, which snaked along beside it. In one house, there was W. E. and his son, W. E. Wells, Jr. In another, lived W. E.'s brother Joseph, and his son, Joseph Wells, Jr., and then, eventually, his son, Joseph Wells III. In yet another house resided W. E.'s other brother, Arthur, and his children. All the Wellses lived and bred and built on the hill, which was dubbed "Newell Heights" by the locals when W. E. erected a Georgian-style mansion complete with drawing rooms and cigar parlors and custom-made moldings inscribed with family crests.

In it, whole rooms were devoted to treasures from far-flung places. One room was lined with blue glass; another was devoted to hunting trophies. Occasionally, cheetah skins could be seen drying on the clothesline, awaiting placement alongside the elephant-foot stools and antler ashtray stands inside the house.

The Wells women had their own diversions—hosting balls and ordering dresses from New York City. Betty Wells, wife of Joe Wells, Jr., came from Akron rubber money. She was raised in a house with butlers and attendants, the rooms wired with floor buttons to summon the help, and so she felt Newell Heights, grand though it was, to be a step down. She and Arthur's wife, Roberta, coped by raising chinchillas in Arthur's basement and spending inordinate amounts of time in bed, eating sweets and reading society magazines.

Other Wells houses followed, until the whole hilltop was mottled with estates of varying size. Their friends included notables from all walks of life. Amelia Earhart was one guest, Solomon Guggenheim another. The Wellses even had a basement room designed by Frank Lloyd Wright. It was a horror of mirrors and stuffed zebra couches, all lighted with blue neon. At the rear, there was a faux fireplace that crackled like crumpled tinfoil. Still, it was created by Frank Lloyd Wright.

Not that anyone in Newell really gave a rat's about Wright or Guggenheim or Earhart. They may have been famous, but they weren't valley folks, which to most valley residents meant they weren't worth paying much notice to. What mattered more to the potters, what really got them out of bed in the morning, were the sports.

All the potteries had teams. Ever competitive, HLC had the best. They developed their own baseball team in 1920. After baseball, they put together football, softball, and basketball teams. Talented athletes often chose to work at HLC simply so they could play ball with the top players. The games were played on Clarke Field (named for an HLC sales manager), which was located on Washington Street, across from the Wells High School football stadium. In 1929, the Wellses installed lights at Clarke Field so the workers could play night games against opponents from farther away. The 1923 football team won the West Virginia Championship, beating teams like Art Rooney's Pittsburgh Steelers. The baseball teams were equally impressive. One 1927 season opener drew a crowd of four thousand.

During the twenties, most potters made better money than they ever expected. Andrew Blair earned enough to buy a car. No one save the pottery owners was getting rich, but no one was starving, either. There was steady work and spare change for the picture show. As President Hoover declared, "The fundamental business of the country, that is production and distribution of commodities, is on a sound and prosperous basis." Photographs were snapped of the potters and salesmen dressed in neckties, slacks, and white bucks tied with neat matching bows. Their hair was parted down the middle and oiled to the sides of their heads. In their hands, they balanced dewy bourbon cocktails and cigarettes.

Group photographs were a pottery tradition, starting as early as the potteries themselves. Potters took pride in their craft, and the photos often showed them lined up like schoolchildren in front of a particularly attractive jug or canister, the factory name propped on a sign in the corner of the frame.

Secure and proud, people flocked to the local parks, rode merry-go-rounds, and ate ice cream. They hit home runs and posed for pictures with the dishware they'd made. They got married and had children and never looked much beyond the valley where they lived. The future was bleached white with promise. The potters were all part of something. They knew, because they could hold it in their hands.

CHAPTER SIX

Ａnd then the bottom fell out.

My grandmother was ten years old when the economy stammered and the Depression began bleeding the confidence from the nation. By 1932, more than 12 million Americans had lost their jobs. As a whole, West Virginians were harder hit simply because they had fewer options. The local economy hinged on factory output, and when the rest of the nation stopped buying, there was little reason for making pottery. In 1932, pottery production dropped to 180 million pieces of ware, from 396 million pieces in 1929, with the national value plummeting from $45 million to $19 million. Workers were lucky to earn twelve dollars a week. The region quickly shifted from the industrial promised land to the stuff of grim black-and-white Appalachian photographs—sickly kids in too-big clothes, women in soiled housedresses, reed-thin men leaning in doorjambs while even thinner dogs gasped at their feet.

What Grandmother hated most about the Depression were the woolen socks. Her woolen socks were thick as her father's thumb and two sizes too large. They bunched and fell into the heel of her shoe, which was a size too small. Walking became a gymnastic exercise, a constant attempt to yank the fallen socks from their crowded puddle without feeling the scrape of wool any more than necessary. All the girls wore woolen socks, rolled down to the ankle for the warm months. They also all wore smocks and had their hair chopped at home, with varying levels of success, in the style of Louise Brooks.

Though frugal, the Blairs quickly burned through what money they had saved, and Aneita Jean was sent down the street to wait in line for yesterday's bread. She would walk the railroad tracks to get there, kicking stones in her path. On the way, she passed soup kitchens, where cans were doled out, one per family. She was never sent to the kitchens. Instead, her twelve-year-old brother, Petey, went down to the river to catch catfish with cornmeal bait. He carried it home in a bucket, and Edna fried it with lard in a cast-iron skillet until it was crisp. Petey wasn't much for fishing; he found it slow. But he was the eldest boy, so it wasn't really up for discussion. To pass the hours, he worked on perfecting his smoke rings, a stunt that never failed to impress the girls.

It was around this time that Andrew Blair took a series of family snapshots. He walked his children to the holler and lined them up on fallen logs. While Edna loved her kids unashamedly, Andrew cared for his children in the same way a rancher does his cattle, and the photo session was more about recording his prize than it was an expression of affection.

In one picture, Petey, Aneita Jean, Forbes, Alan, and Nancy stand in a line, then appear side by side in another. There is Alan by himself on the log, then Petey, Aneita, and Alan together on the log. And so it goes, all of Andrew's children wearing their churchgoing clothes, huddled together for posterity.

Alan and Nancy barely register, being so young and bundled up. Forbes never seems to look directly at the lens. Aneita Jean looks forward, but her embarrassment is palpable, and in one shot, she hides behind her knee. Petey is, as ever, the exception.

Though only a boy, he radiates certitude. He points at the camera, mugs, and sucks in his cheeks. He is more alive than all of them combined. In one photograph, he reaches toward the lens, fingers splayed, brow furrowed, and tongue tucked, fearless and hungry, grasping for life with the appetite of a grown man who believes himself immune to circumstance.

Indeed, a few years later, Pete would become the ringleader of the upper-end gang, even though he himself was a low-ender, nearly a Newellie. The gang wasn't a gang as such. They were just a bunch of boys loaded with mischief and free time. They raced cars, drank liquor, and threw stones at tin cans. Bull's-eye! There was a lot of talk about baseball and getting laid. One of the first things Petey did as leader was dig a thirty-foot tunnel under the buxom upper-ender Nancy Logan's house and entice her down there to play hide-and-seek. This endeavor alone ensured his popularity for years to come.

In time, the Depression sucked the life out of the family. Andrew grew nastier, Edna more weary. People still stopped on the front porch, but there was no cake and less kidding around. Jokes took on an anxious tone, and the laughter that followed them was slab-sided and stilted. Panic-strung faces were tight with worry until hopelessness drew them down, the skin sinking inward like water disappearing into dirt. Men drank more and beat their families with displaced wrath. People took to stealing pottery from the dump, carting home off-center plates and chipped glasses, loading up on ware that only months before they had pridefully tossed out as unworthy.

"The town went to wrack and ruin," my grandmother says.

HLC pressed on. It built another plant and capitalized on the desperate labor. Rock Springs Park still operated, but fewer folks rode the merry-go-round, and those who did found little excitement in the trip.

Edna began spending more time at Mrs. Gotchel's house. Mrs. Gotchel was a medium who lived across the street. A bony crimp of a woman, Mrs. Gotchel read fortunes and ran numbers from her back porch. Edna went to her for both. She believed in ghosts. She wasn't sure what had started her believing, only that it seemed improbable to her that what she saw was all there was in the world, an instinct Mrs. Gotchel would happily, for a nickel, confirm.

When Edna got pregnant for the first time, she consulted Mrs. Gotchel about what sex her baby would be and whether or not it would be healthy. She was anxious because she hadn't conceived until she was thirty-two, too old, she thought. Mrs. Gotchel told her she saw a son, but that there was a shadow of doom attached to him. She said he would cost Edna something. So when Edna gave birth to Petey Dink and her beloved dog Blossom ran away, she was not surprised. She considered her nickel well spent.

A few weeks later, they found Blossom, bloated and stiff, underneath a white oak. "Old age," said Andrew. But Edna knew the animal had died from a broken heart, and that was the reason she gave whenever anybody inquired as to where Blossom had gone.

Aneita Jean liked the Blossom story and made her mother tell it repeatedly. In the memory book, there is a photograph of Blossom curled in Edna's arms. Edna is sitting cross-legged in the grass; barefoot and sun-streaked, she is wearing a housedress. On her lap, Blossom naps like an infant, his brown head propped up, his eyes narrowed into slits of ecstasy.

Aneita Jean wanted a dog of her own, but her father said they had too many mouths to feed as it was, and so she settled for the picture, sticking it in the frame of her bedroom mirror.

During the Depression, one of the mouths being fed belonged to Edna's mother, Mewey, a woman who possessed a gift for irritating and turning weekend visits into monthlong stays.

Mewey didn't do much but plant herself in Andrew's leather chair and chatter orders to her daughter and her grandkids.

"How about bringing me an orange juice, Jeannie?"

"How about lifting them blinds?"

"How about something to nibble on? Old lady going to starve to death in this house."

Every night after dinner, Mewey would unknot her bun and let her hair tumble down the back of the leather chair. Aneita Jean would sit behind the chair and comb each strand, careful not to tug too hard. The hair was coarse, gray, and so long that it pooled on the floor.

While Aneita Jean combed, Mewey would tell her stories about old West Virginia. About mountain men and wild Indians and how the whole landscape was riddled with poisonous snakes. How children went to schools in shacks, if they went at all. And how even back then there was clay all along the Monongahela River and that people fashioned it into jugs and bowls, and eventually bricks, which were shipped to Pittsburgh to build that city.

"You know to make bone china, they char actual bones in the kilns? Used to do that in East Liverpool, but it made such a stink, they stopped. No one makes real bone china anymore."

She talked about the roads back then, or the want of them, and how travel was almost impossible, but that people did anyway, especially for preaching.

"Reverends would preach outside and folks would sit on saw boards propped with pin legs. People wouldn't dress as they do now. Instead, they'd wear moccasins and hunting clothes and their guns would be loaded and at the ready just in case of Indian attack. After the preaching, everyone would eat and then walk back home, up to twenty miles away."

"Did you walk that far, Grandmother?"

"Lord, child, you think I'm so old? I feel about a hundred years old, but I went to a proper church."

As Aneita Jean combed, Mewey continued, growing more dramatic with each tale, the momentum of the storytelling causing her neck to tighten and flush.

"Sometimes on these walks home, the pioneers would be set upon by Indians and shot, scalped, and mutilated. No matter how hospitable the whites were to them, they stayed savages. Sometimes they'd drop coins or silver on the trail and then attack when the settlers bent to pick them up. Wily bastards, those Indians."

"They wouldn't scalp girls, would they?"

"Lord yes. They'd scalp anybody, knock their brains out against a barn board. No better than thieves. Kill you for a bucket of syrup."

On and on she went, regaling her granddaughter with stories. Aneita Jean combed Mewey's hair until it snapped with electricity.

"Where are the Indians now, Grandmother?"

"Dead, like they deserve."

Andrew didn't like Mewey filling his girl's head with stories.

"She wants stories, she should read."

"A girl can't read all the time," Mewey would snip back. "Make her dull. Like you."

Mewey was one of the only people who ever talked back to Andrew. When she did it, Aneita Jean would sit frozen and wait. Nothing ever happened, although each time she still feared something would. Her father just narrowed his lips into a line and slammed the door on his way out to the studio. Mewey would issue a little "Humph," hitch her hips, and settle back into the leather chair, picking up the stories where she'd left off.

CHAPTER SEVEN

Puberty hit my grandmother like a dropped piano.
  She got her period when she was twelve, while watching one of the pottery variety shows.

  "I was there alone with my father," she says. "He wanted to take me to the hospital."

The effect was akin to pulling a rip cord. Out came the breasts and the bum and the awareness that there were so many eyes on her, it made her skin hot.

At twelve, Aneita Jean was too young to understand why they looked, and too young to know what such attention would mean, how it would stick to her like tar and rob her head of any subjects beyond hemlines and brassieres, or how, over time, those stares would become so familiar, so expected, that the thought of surviving without them would drain her chest of air.

"I was built like Miss America. It's the damn truth."

Aneita Jean's class picture from this time shows her squinting and skeptical in the second row. Her head is cocked to the left, her arms locked behind her. Her brow is knit. The other girls are straight-faced, trying to look proper. Only one is smiling, and in truth she looks a little slow. The faces of the boys are not much different. They, too, are affecting stature, chins down, arms limp at their sides, bow ties knotted tightly around their sapling necks.

Aneita Jean watched the older girls Petey Dink brought home, saw how they crossed their legs at the ankles and tugged at their garters when they thought no one was looking. She learned that presence required diligence—a sock folded just so, rouge reapplied in the reflection of a chrome bumper. She watched the girls in her class, saw them struggling with their own unexpected visibility, or, worse, with the horrible knowledge that they weren't being observed at all.

"Life is exhausting work, girl," Mewey had told her once when she caught Aneita Jean fussing over her hair. "Don't borrow trouble."

But she was growing up. She did not know how to stop

herself from feeling things. She was already becoming one of those women who attract men. Women whose every movement is watched and savored and who unfurl them-selves to it like flags. And since she was built like Miss America, it wasn't really her choice to make.

Photographs record the rapid change. The girl with the fierce scowl becomes the girl with the apologetic eyes, becomes the girl with the sly smile, becomes the girl with the fetching head tilt, becomes the girl with her skirt blown up to her garters. As you flip the pages, the transformation appears so obvious, so fateful, that if you flip fast enough, it almost self-animates, like those old paper cartoons of a dog chasing its tail. The Kewpie eyes and lascivious mouth, once premature, begin to look at home on her wide white face. Her red hair grows from a flat pageboy cut into a wilder flip awry with curls. Her figure pops, well on its way to its eventual 36-24-36 dimensions.

The impact of her new body was immediate, rushing her into the eyeteeth of the valley boys. Men took heed well before it was proper for them to do so.

Andrew Blair noticed. Mostly, he noticed how other men responded to his daughter. How their eyes jigged after her when she tottered down the street. How they strained to catch her attention: "Hey, Jeannie! Over here, Jeannie!"

So sudden was her transformation that her father forced her to wear a pink sack dress passed on from the neighbors. A rectangle of fabric, it somehow managed to be tight around the collar and wide everywhere else. Buttons big as saucers adorned the upper portion, running from collar to waist and commanding attention away from any other part of the garment or wearer. Andrew also felt the impetus to drag Aneita Jean into the cellar, put his hand below her throat, and yell, "Now look, no man will ever touch you from here down, you hear?" He was, of course, wrong.

•

Like everyone else in Hancock County, Aneita Jean knew a few things about Frank Willis.

She knew he loved animals. That he kept a whole penful of bunnies in his backyard, darling white and gray longeared rabbits hopping and lolling in the shade of his house. She knew that his father was a potter and that his mother was a checkout woman at a department store in East Liverpool. She knew Frank didn't work, or didn't keep jobs anyhow. That he'd been fired from HLC and Harker and that now he held a shift at the mill, feeding lumber into the planer piece by ragged piece. And she knew that when people spoke about Frank, their eyes always darted around as if they were looking for lost change.

Frank lived down the road from the Blairs, in his parents' house, even though he was in his twenties and should have been off and married long ago. Aneita Jean usually took her time walking past Frank's house because she was crazy for the bunnies. Sometimes she'd see Frank working in the yard, mending the pen or maybe just digging in the dirt, and she would wave hello like her mother said she should.

Frank didn't wave back, didn't pay her much mind at all, until one day, when he saw her lingering by the rabbits and asked if she might do him a favor.

"You Andrew Blair's kid, ain'tcha?"

"Yes, sir."

"How would you like to go to the store for me? I'm

busy here and am nearly starving. You go off and bring me some bologna and I'll let you hold one," he said, jerking his head toward the pen.

Aneita Jean smiled. She knew just the one she wanted to pet, the little white one in the corner.

Frank handed her some money and off she went, running to the market and back. When she returned, Frank waved her inside and pointed toward the fridge.

"Your mother works at Olgivies, doesn't she?" Aneita Jean asked as she unloaded the lunch meat and the white bread.

"Yup."

"I put your cold cuts on the second shelf," she said.

"Think you could do me another favor?" Frank was at the sink, his back to her.

Aneita Jean walked up to him, stood alongside the sink, and peered inside.

"Think you could hold this for a minute?"

And with that, he swiveled, his semierect penis cradled in his chapped hands.

She froze. Frank worked quickly, rubbing himself up and down, until with a shriek he jerked back to the sink and ejaculated into the basin.

My grandmother doesn't remember leaving. Just the sink, and his work shirt and sweater, how they smelled of sap, and the gleam of the enamel counter, and the vision of his mother ringing up nylons at Olgivies.

•

In the mountains, fortunes change as quickly as the weather. Sometimes you can see the fog curling in, but most times you're caught unawares, the darkness snapping like a blind over the sky.

There were more men after Frank Willis. Men who saw a girl who looked like a woman and couldn't stop themselves, men who obeyed their urges as if they were directives from God.

My grandmother blanches when she thinks about what happened. These are unsavory topics, subjects best left behind. She struggles for a better memory, one vivid enough to squelch the others.

"One time, these two bears fought to the death in Newell Park," she says.

In Newell Park, there was a zoo with a questionable menagerie, founded on the dreams of George Clarke, an HLC salesman and frustrated zookeeper who was the park's supervisor until he suffered a heart attack during a sales trip out west.

Built in 1905, the park housed bears, seals, monkeys, birds, and all manner of other animals that Clarke had wrangled from other, more traditional zoos. There were also walking paths and gardens and an outdoor theater that hosted orchestras. It was an ideal picnic spot for potters and a popular place to spend lazy Sundays ogling the wildlife living, weirdly, improbably, a short stroll from a pottery factory in Newell.

The bear fight started with a roar that carved through the holler like a train, a great rush of hell that called men out from the pottery and women from their homes. Children fled the schools and lined up along the holler roads, where they could just make out the battle below. Pottery workers had already encircled the cage ten deep. Word spread so quickly that the trolleys from East Liverpool became jammed with people hoping to make it to the park before the drama ended.

Inside the cage, the two bears, a male and a female, were standing, mouths pulled back, teeth wet, roaring at each other with a force that vibrated their heads and shook their necks. Their fur fanned out, damp with sweat. They circled and stood, circled and stood, and then the female charged, biting the male's throat. He pawed back, slicing her jowls open. Undeterred, she heaved into his chest, biting wildly. The crowd began to cheer.

The bears fought for several hours, until the female, weary and outweighed, sunk to the cage floor and died. The fight over, the potters returned to their shifts, the women went home to start supper, and the children grudgingly slunk back to school.

CHAPTER EIGHT

During the Depression, my grandmother and her brothers spent as much time as possible outdoors. They chased rats at the pottery dump. They picked elderberries and built lean-tos out of leaves and branches. They skipped stones and waded in the river. They played pussy in the corner and button, button, who's got the button? and lots and lots of cards. They did all those things that in retrospect seem quaint and out of a storybook but that at the time were just things to do, free stuff that took them away from the gloomy adults and killed the hours.

Nancy was still a baby then, but Aneita Jean was told to watch her, and so she did, carrying her to the river to sit at the shoreline. Her father forbade her to go there, but her mother said it was fine, that kids needed fresh air, and so off they went, a twelve-year-old and a toddler, cutting a path to the river's edge.

One day, they found an old canoe. Aneita Jean hollered for some boys to help her flip it over, and together they launched it into the Ohio. The bottom was full of mold, so they decided to flip it over like a hideout and swim underneath.

The upturned canoe floated just fine, and soon Aneita Jean and a whole mess of boys were bobbing beneath it, their heads knocking together like billiard balls. They were only under for a couple of minutes, but it was enough, because by the time Aneita Jean remembered Nancy, her baby sister was gone.

Aneita Jean swam to shore and screamed for help. Screamed less from loss than from fear of retribution. Her sister was gone, she wailed. A baby. Gone. The whole pack of kids searched until dusk, lifting brush and upturning rocks, fearing the worst.

My grandmother remembers walking the edge of the river, shaking from cold and panic, wondering what she would do if Nancy were really gone. She decided she could never go home, and that she would paddle that leaky canoe as far away as she could, until she, too, drowned.

It was then that she heard a yelp. A boy had found Nancy sunk into a hole not six feet from where Aneita Jean had left her. She was chilled, white, and glassy-eyed, but she was alive.

Aneita Jean never confessed what had happened by the river. She said they were late because they had lost track of time. For that, she got a whipping from her father and a doubtful glance from her mother, who knew better.

Andrew's fury did not ebb with his daughter's castigation. He punished Edna the next day.

Just beyond the porch, near Edna's chair, was a delicate flowering tree, a tree of heaven. When the wind blew, Edna thought the leaves sounded like murmuring, like voices from the past calling to her.

"Listen there," she'd say. "Hear that?"

Edna spent hours gazing toward her tree, thinking it more beautiful than any flower. The tree pleased her, and it was because of this as much as anything that the day after she sent Aneita Jean and Nancy to the river, her husband took an ax and cut it down.

"It's too messy," he said. "I'm sick of looking at it."

Aneita Jean ran inside to her mother, who was watching her husband from the window as he whacked time and again at the tender bark, his necktie flailing like a scarf with each blow.

"I'm sorry, Mother," she cried. And she was, for the tree, for Nancy, for Frank Willis, for being so ugly inside.

•

There was a rock as big as a house in the middle of the Ohio River. The rock sat a few yards out and was flat as cheese. It was an irresistible temptation for the boys of the valley, being perfect for racing to and diving off of.

When Aneita Jean and her brother Petey Dink weren't stealing apples or walking the Lincoln Highway into East Liverpool, they'd be at the river, swimming out to that rock, which they dubbed "Bare Butt Beach," because when the boys swam there alone, they inevitably ended up naked, their jerky adolescent movements mimicking the jut and collapse of the rocks around them.

Aneita Jean adored Bare Butt Beach. She didn't care that the rats there were large as beavers. Or that it was the preferred location for the factory workers to use the bathroom. Emerging from the pottery, they would carry two-by-fours with holes cut in the center, which they propped in between two trees and perched on like crows. She liked to spy on the naked boys, to stare at their silly things swinging like pole beans as they dived into the river. She hid out in the trees, straddling a branch, rapt for hours while the boys, these slack-assed, swivel-hipped boys with narrow shoulders, muscles rounded like river stones, anxious faces, bulging trousers, and the manic energy of a litter of puppies, raced, chased, and tackled one another to within an inch of their lives.

When she wasn't peeping, she was at the shoreline, flirting with the very boys she'd already seen in the buff. She swam in her mother's pantaloons, the legs filled with air and bobbing like beer barrels around her tiny hips.

There was a rope swing just to the left of Bare Butt Beach, and Petey Dink swung farther than any of the other guys, his overall braces flapping in the breeze. Unlike his friends, who grew spotty and sullen with age, Petey Dink became more bewitching during adolescence. His arms were now sinewy and vinelike; his mouth had widened and pushed his cheeks ever higher. His forehead was broad, and he wore his hair slicked back. He dressed in flat-front pants, his shirt tucked in, his tie skimming his waistline. When he raised his long arms, his jacket sleeves would pull up short, as if he were expanding right before your eyes.

Like all Blairs, Petey Dink stood up straight, making him appear even taller than six four. At rest, Petey kept his shoulders square and turned his left knee out. As kids, he and Aneita Jean shared a bedroom, and at night she would pray that someday she would meet a man just like him. A man who whispered in girls' ears, making them blush. A man who smoked on street corners and drank from paper bags. A man who was always laughing and made everyone else laugh, too. My grandmother noticed that Petey, unlike some men, wasn't selfish. He shared airtime, doled it out in equal parts, which he didn't have to do, because everyone would have been content just to stand in his circle and watch his handsome, brimming face.

"What do you think?" he'd query everyone from the paperboy to the trolley driver.

"Suppose it'll rain?"

"What do you think?"

"Any chance the president will pull the country out?"

"What do you think?"

"Petey, are you trying to seduce me?"

"What do you think?"

Aneita Jean loved Petey because he could dance, because at fifteen he wouldn't drop her hand, not even when his buddies from school walked by. When he took a stroll, she skipped alongside. When he went to relieve himself behind a tree, she peeked through the chinks of her fingers. Aneita Jean became a human tick firmly attached to the underbelly of her oldest brother, and, lucky for her, he had the good grace not to mind. When she would tell him her plans about leaving, about becoming a painter, he would listen and smile, then say, "That sure sounds good to me."

The local ladies nicknamed him "Plenty Bad," a moniker he relished. Throughout high school, he seduced legions of girls, a staggering number, leading many folks to speculate that there probably wasn't a skirt left in the valley that Petey Dink hadn't peered under. He mysteriously got *A*'s, even though he never went to class. He was given the thickest slice of pie at every bake sale, even church bake sales, especially at church bake sales. He told all the girls he met that Blair was Scottish for "make a loud noise," and that they'd better cover their ears. He used corny lines and misquoted poetry, and got away with both.

Many of the girls he dated were, in fact, women, years older, but still unable to resist his angled cheeks and unfettered hips. He'd turn back flips like an acrobat, and the girls would swoon, gasping as he plunked heels-down onto the grass. "Ornery" is what his mother called him, especially when he'd come home damp and numb from swimming in the river.

In the memory book, Petey Dink looks the same in all the pictures. Petey Dink on the top of the train. Petey Dink behind a veil of sweet peas. Petey Dink in the holler, at school, smoking with his friends, in the yard, his hands behind his back and a dirty smirk on his face.

When he was fifteen, he dated Elaine Riley, a silent-movie star, famous, at least as far as West Virginia was concerned. She was elusive and dark, and the two of them would hop trains together, necking in the empty cars as they rattled toward Pittsburgh.

"I love you, Laney," he'd say over the clatter of the boxcar hinges.

"You love everyone, Petey," she'd shoot back, tossing her cigarette into the wind.

Pete would laugh, then sweep in, arms, chest, then the whole weight of him bearing down and shaking with his own self-satisfied giggles, as Elaine breathed him in, all vanilla and pressed grass. Together, they'd watch the mountains clip by, little snapshots between the cars, blinks of life growing darker and darker.

Petey had been jumping trains for as long as he could walk. The Universal Crane line would rumble through town daily, loading up on coal and pottery, and Petey would make a point of leaping on board just as it heaved over the bridge. When the trains were in the yard, he'd walk the tops like sidewalks, his arms held straight above his head, his slim fingers stretched toward the sky.

Like his mother, he never let on that he was sick. Aneita Jean knew. She had heard her parents whisper about it once late at night in their bedroom.

"The boy needs to simmer down," her father said. "Not going to last like he's doing now."

She remembers how that word *last* had hitched in her ear, a barb.

Petey Dink had been born with a hole in his heart. It was a minute gap, like a prick from a nail, but it was enough to send the doctors into fits of worry and to warn the Blairs that if nothing else, Petey Dink should stay as sedentary as possible. Activity made his heart flutter. But Petey wasn't made for stillness. He was jittery by nature, wiry, and forever tapping his foot or snapping his fingernail against his belt loop. Watching him, you got the feeling that if he stopped fidgeting, he would cease to be. Sometimes in bed after a nightmare, he'd swear he could hear his heart gurgle, feel the muscle slamming against his chest as if it were trying to escape. It was the same feeling he got when he was making love, and while it frightened him, it also made him feel alive. Giving up swimming was one thing. Giving up women was something else.

One night, Aneita Jean awoke to find Petey Dink standing atop his bed, arching his shoulders back, eyes still thick with sleep. She screamed as he dived headfirst into the wood floor. His skull made an awful thud, sending a ripple through the bed. She threw back the blankets and scrambled to his side. He was snoring lightly, a half smile on his face, as ever, unfazed.

•

Throughout junior high and high school, Aneita Jean's best friend was a girl named Stella Weaver. Stella lived across the street from the Blairs and called my grandmother "Jeannie," like everybody else did. Aneita Jean called Stella "Snook," for no real reason she can remember.

Snook was one of the few girls Aneita Jean could count on as a friend. Other girls didn't want much to do with her. There was Sara Hocking, of course, but she liked everybody. And a handful of others whom she went to the corner store with to buy suckers and Cokes. But she didn't trust them. She always felt that they were whispering about her the minute she turned her back, about who did she think she was, about her mama. Snook was different.

Snook was a quiet girl with long, narrow eyes and a thick nose that hung over her mouth. Because the Weavers both worked in the pottery, Snook was alone pretty much all the time. She and Aneita Jean became inseparable, sisters who played pretend and spun jacks, who ran behind the trolley or walked along the Ohio picking weeds, arms swinging and fingers linked together like a chain.

Snook was an only child, so sometimes she'd visit Jeannie's house and marvel at the boys, Petey Dink and Forbes and Alan Mead. More often, though, the two girls would hole up in Snook's empty house and imagine it was theirs.

When Snook's parents did come home after their shifts, it was never for long. Her father had a temper, and her mother found it best to take him to the Legion, where he could have a bourbon and clink glasses with his buddies from the pottery. When the Weavers came home from their nights at the dance hall, Mr. Weaver would call Aneita Jean over.

"Come here, little Jeannie. Come give me a hug. What are you, thirteen now? Look old for your age, don't ya?"

Aneita Jean would walk slowly, dragging her feet across the floor as if they were numb. When she finally made her way to his chair, he'd shoot his arm out and yank her to his chest, as if he were snagging a fish with a net. She would stiffen and he would hug harder.

"I bet you're a ticklish little girl, aren't you?" he'd say, moving his thin fingers over her back. "Does this tickle?" Aneita Jean would wriggle free, pretending to laugh, and run back to Snook, who never watched her daddy except out of the corner of her eye.

Sometimes, Snook would be hauled to the Legion with her folks and left to sit in a corner chair while her mom and dad drank their fill. When that happened, Aneita Jean would sneak over to the Weavers' house and go into the master bedroom. She'd open the closet, see Mr. Weaver's trousers there on the floor, limp and oily, still reeking of Legion smoke. And she would dig her hands in his pockets and steal the change.

The next day, as she and Snook passed the corner grocery, she'd pause. "How about some chocolate, Snook?" she'd ask.

•

My grandmother had only one other close childhood friend. Paddy lived by the river. No one saw where he slept, but Aneita Jean imagined it was in a tree house or a little hut he'd built from fallen branches. Paddy was exceptionally clean. He must have bathed in the Ohio. He never stank or showed signs of living as he did in the elements, except he did have rough skin, weathered like the side of a barn. He also had a thick, sagging neck, which he tried to hide by pressing his chin into his chest. His smile was warm and his manner gentle. Most days, he lumbered up and down the river's edge at dawn; then as the sun came up, he'd find a sturdy rock and sit down with his pocketknife to carve. His specialty was making tiny boats from buckeyes.

Aneita Jean sat with him sometimes on the cool of the rocks, watching as he peeled the buckeyes clean with the knife's edge, never crushing them, even though his hands were large as dinner plates. The nutshells would all but disappear in the folds of his fingers, then reemerge like a fish tossed in the surf.

They didn't speak much. Paddy would give her a completed boat, she would thank him, and then he would nod once and pick up the next shell. She kept them all in her top dresser drawer, where they sailed atop a sea of love letters, scarves, and photographs of James Cagney and Clark Gable.

•

At school, Snook and Aneita Jean often ran into Petey and his best friend, George Kelly. George and Petey palled around and hunted together. They chased girls and drank themselves silly. They were fifteen-year-old boys, imprudent, indecent, immortal.

After class, all four of them would lounge on the hill in front of their wide redbrick schoolhouse, making predictions about classmates—"Dime says he's going to trip on the curb"—and playing worse fate.

"Lose a leg or lose an arm?"

"Arm."

"Arm."

"Aneita Jean, what do you think?"

"Leg. You can't hug with one arm."

"Yeah, but you can't dance with one leg, 'less you want to dance like Georgie here."

"Good one, Pete."

My grandmother knew George was in love with Petey by the way he hovered around, hanging off his shoulder and laughing uneasily at all his jokes. Something smelled desperate about George, and it was because of this as much as anything that Aneita Jean was wary of him. Still, he was Petey's best friend. And he played the trumpet in the Chester High School band, and the other girls seemed to like him all right. So when he invited her to come see his ceramic dog collection, and Edna said it was okay, she went.

Aneita Jean trailed George upstairs to his bedroom, where he kept the dogs. As she climbed the stairs, she noticed that the back of his neck was sweaty.

"Ta da!" he said, swinging open the door and pushing Aneita Jean toward the dresser, where a pack of ceramic dogs in various acts of sleeping, barking, and pointing sat carefully lined up in a semicircle.

"Look here, Jeannie," he said, tugging her dress sleeve and shoving her toward a separate dog displayed on his bedside table. The dog was urinating, it's spindly ceramic leg delicately lifted toward George's dresser mirror. Aneita Jean laughed nervously, the sound bouncing down the hall. George edged toward her. She took a step back, feeling the cool metal of the bed frame against her calves.

"Be quiet," George hissed. "Be quiet." But she couldn't. That dog was dirty and she was in a boy's bedroom and he was standing close to her, close enough to smell the tuna from his lunch when he leaned down and said, "Be quiet, you stupid girl."

Later, back on the porch, snug next to her mother in the wicker chair, Aneita Jean glanced over to George's house, up to his bedroom window, and she saw him there, motionless, his penis squashed against the glass.

She looked at Edna, but her eyes were closed. And so Aneita Jean closed hers, too.

It happened the first time in June. Aneita Jean was thirteen, old enough to have been baby-sitting at a neighbor's party. She put the baby down to sleep upstairs, then wandered down to the living room, where the festivities were in full swing. She walked past the baked chicken and potato salad, past the tipsy women sitting on the laps of men who weren't their husbands, past the men smoking and telling tales about the pottery boss's delicate stomach.

She sneaked outside to the stone wall that edged the lawn and sat down, breathing deeply. She sat there a good while, staring at the milk white moon, the dull jab of the stones pressing into her bum while the distant laughter of grown-ups swirled around her like a protective blanket. She sat there calm and easy, unaware that she was being watched.

The party grew louder, and Aneita Jean knew she'd better get back inside and check on the baby. She hopped down, crept back inside, and climbed the stairs. The baby was sleeping that scary still-baby sleep, so Aneita Jean lay down on the quilt next to her and nuzzled close enough to hear her breathe. She put her hand over the baby's chest and felt the cool wet of baby skin on her palm.

She awoke to the sound of the door creaking open. She could tell from the backlit outline that it was not the baby's mother who was coming in, but a boy. She said nothing, pressed her eyes shut, and pretended she was still asleep. When the boy climbed on top of her, she knew who it was. Silently, she slid the baby to the far corner of the blanket, until only her fingertips were touching the baby's chubby thigh. Then she lay absolutely still while George Kelly ran his shaky hands over her belly and under her dress.

•

In the album, there are many photographs of my grand-mother with other women's babies. She was baby-crazy then, hungering for their innocence, sick with their sweet scent. When she looks at these photographs now, she remembers not the children, but what happened when she was watching them. How George Kelly would find her and drop by to "use the phone."

"I always told him he couldn't use the phone," she says. "That it wasn't mine to give. I was thirteen. What could I do?"

She remembers how her heart would stutter and spurt when he rapped at the screen door. How she would keep her eyes on the children while he kissed her and hurriedly worked his way beneath her clothes. When he was done, he would walk to the phone and call his high school girlfriend, "a pretty girl who felt lucky George had chosen her."

My grandmother won't discuss the rest. How her heart withered and she felt scrambled inside. How she was only thirteen when it started and seventeen when it finally stopped. How she knew, because it happened so often, that she must deserve it—"I *was* built like Miss America."

No. All she says is that "it was awful." But then, no one escapes awful. "Sooner or later, everyone is in for a world of hurt." My grandmother lived in West Virginia. Hurt was everywhere.

CHAPTER NINE

In the thirties, HLC introduced a line of china called Virginia Rose, named after W. E. Wells's granddaughter.
More than 150 decorations were used on the pottery—four
sprigs, no line; one sprig, silver edge line; seven sprigs, silver
edge, verge border, et cetera. In 1936, a thirty-two-piece set
sold for eleven dollars.

The same year, Aneita Jean Blair turned sixteen years old and was drowning in her looks. Maybe it was her father. Or maybe it was Frank Willis or George Kelly. Maybe it was the valley, or the factories. Or maybe it was just because she was born ugly and then stopped being ugly so suddenly, her body ripening before her brain, that beauty had become oxygen to her. It was the one thing she knew she possessed that had value beyond the pottery, beyond West Virginia, and she had come to understand the language implicitly. She knew what the glimpse of a slip did to men, how to catch your hips when you walked. She taught herself these things, studying Bette Davis movies and Hollywood gossip magazines, although most of it she knew innately; most of it had been stamped into her genetic code from the get-go and was just awaiting activation, like a match to a bottle rocket.

Boys began calling. So many boys. To amuse herself in high school, Aneita Jean decided she would woo as many men as possible. She devoted herself to soliciting their attentions and began to crave those tickles that flushed her cheeks, those spidery torments she didn't yet have a name for. Attracting men made her feel powerful. Her father, abandoned and besieged, took to beating her nightly with a belt.

At any given time, Aneita Jean would be dating at least three boys, usually more like five, and she would keep it all aboveboard, telling each man about the others, then watch as it drove them to lunacy.

Seeing men fight over her became a routine event. "Ought to have sold tickets," she says. "Be a rich woman now."

Edna tried to help, told her, "Pretty is as pretty does," but Aneita Jean didn't really believe it. She knew pretty was teased hair and tight sweaters, milky skin and ankles thin as celery stalks. Problem was, in the valley, chasing beauty was putting on airs, inviting trouble. Beauty was poisonous because it manufactured hope. Hope gave people dreams, and dreams had a way of turning what was once a perfectly acceptable way of life into a blinding prison, like the ax strike that floods light into a mine shaft.

In the valley, the only beauty you could get away with was pretty-sweet, like Sara Hocking, a neighbor down the road, who also had a steady stream of men calling on her.

"I would see them pass by my house," says Grandmother. "They loved Sara. To a point."

Sara had a shock of black hair and a slicey smile. She was voted the most popular girl in high school, an honor she was sure she didn't deserve. Sara was short but thin, and she stood up straight, taking care to keep her shoulders soft. Her expressions were limited to surprise, gratitude, and delight. She never laughed too loudly. And she didn't question her abilities, which, though limited, she believed in absolutely.

There are a few photographs where my grandmother tries to pull off pretty-sweet. Her lips are pulled back, her nose is wrinkly, and her head is tilted. She looks more like a freshly trapped fox than Sara Hocking. She must have studied these photos herself and seen the unsatisfactory results, because she gave up on pretty-sweet in short order and went for glamour. This, too, was problematic. Girls in the valley weren't bred to be glamorous, but to acquiesce, please, and smile graciously at whatever dabs of pleasure life tossed their way. Which didn't stop them from wanting something more, of aching for it like they would for a mouthful of cake.

"I was who I was. I didn't know how to be different."

By the time she was sixteen, Aneita Jean didn't care who knew her desires. She refused to stuff them down inside her belly and seal them shut behind clamped teeth. So she laughed, hollered, wept. She shook her hair loose, stuck her neck out, and threw her head back with enough force to swell the veins in her throat. She leered and shimmied and posed for photographs with her legs akimbo. She kept her nails polished, painted her lips a hawkish red. She was a dancing scream. And she could watch a boy roll his sleeve and know by the way his fingers slid over the fabric the level of his desire.

Sometimes Aneita Jean feigned illness. The only thing better than being glamorous was being sick. Being sick was like being anointed. There was drama in illness. Swooning and fever put a sprinkle of hallucinatory magic over the dinge of routine. She understood the power of frailty. Nothing made you the center of attention faster than illness, and so she was sick a lot. She was also overcome by many things. Like crossing streams ("I couldn't possibly"), or lifting objects ("Darling, could you?"), or heat ("My goodness, I must lie down"). There was a lot of lying down in Aneita Jean's life.

Petey Dink watched his sister's antics with bemusement. She reminded him of the stars he saw in the movies, sexy and conspicuous, even though she was still a kid. They were both in high school now, she a sophomore, he a senior, and not a day went by that a classmate didn't ask him whom his sister was dating.

"How much time you got?" he'd answer.

"I kept a stash of Hollywood photographs in my dresser," Grandmother says. "Black-and-white photos of Janet Gaynor and Rita Hayworth and Jean Harlow and

Myrna Loy. Oh, and Clara Bow. I couldn't forget her. I wanted to be her so badly."

"At that time, women were looked down upon," she says dryly. "The men were to be pleased; that's what I gathered up."

So Aneita Jean did what so many young girls do when pressed into the service of men too early. She became what she thought they already saw.

•

There are stacks of photographs of my grandmother's beaux in the memory book, so many that their combined thickness strains the binder. The men are generally pictured hamming it up, or staring longingly off the page, or, when shot with Aneita Jean, gazing longingly at her. When she looks at these photographs, my grandmother's breath quickens. Not because of the men, but because when she sees herself in her platform shoes and scarf, in her Capri pants and sandals, in her gold bathing costume, in her cuffed short shorts, she sees a girl in her glory, on the most promising days of her life, before decisions were made and courses set and heartbreaks suffered. In the memory book, my grandmother is in tune. She looks the way she feels.

The men, handsome, preening, thirsty with lust—well, they're just props, props with lungs. In point of fact, most boys bored her after an hour. It was draining to be adored. At least it was when she was sixteen and the whole Ohio River valley was waiting for an opportunity to hold her hand.

Grandmother flips through the pages and narrates with an odd formality, as if her conquests were exhibits.

"Here now is a picture of David Moore," she says.

David is wearing government-issue khaki pants and a khaki two-pocket shirt, the sleeves rolled up to his biceps, which were, despite his job as a government laborer, small as chipmunks. A wide-brimmed hat clings for its life to the back of his head. His boots are loosely laced and riddled with holes. At his feet, a penned inscription: "To the sweetest girl in the world, Love, David." Which shows how little David knew about Aneita Jean.

"He was my first love."

She was twelve and he a bit older. He had doe eyes, jug ears, and an easy smile. He was cute, not handsome, a squatty, bowlegged boy with ragged fingernails and jangly intentions. He lived in Martin's Ferry, West Virginia, which was quite a haul down the mountains just to visit a girl, even if she was the sweetest in the world.

On dates, he and Aneita Jean would sit outside in the yard, legs overlapped, while she colored in the holes on his boots with ink. When he kissed her good-bye, she kept her lips closed and her eyes open.

And then it was over. David climbed back up the mountains in his holey shoes, and she went back to being Aneita Jean Blair from Chester, a bony girl alone in the world, coiled and itchy in her skin.

•

H*ere now is a picture of Howard Walton.*
"I went to the senior prom with Howard Walton; he was my sailor."

The two met at Bertha Andrew's pie party. It went like this: The girls baked their best pies. The boys would sample them, one after another, forkful after forkful. Then the boys would choose a girl based on the succulence of her baked goods.

"I went to the party," says Grandmother. "But I didn't bring a damn pie." No matter. Howard chose her anyway, and the big man with the rectangular build and "the devil in his eye" fell crazy in love.

He courted her for seven years, which was kind of sad, because he never got anywhere. Lord knows, he tried. He dressed to the nines on dates, donning double-breasted suits and shiny ties. He wore a pocket square and slicked his coarse curly hair back on the sides of his wide head. He took Aneita Jean ice-skating and horseback riding and to the picture show. He took her for drives in the holler, past fields of wild strawberries. He held her hand in his thick palm and carried her when she grew weary of walking. And then, once he got a job as a roller in the mill, "a good-money job," he did what all valley boys with good-money jobs did: He proposed.

A photograph from that day shows the happy couple sitting atop the rear bumper of his car on Phoenix Avenue. Howard's legs are spread open and his thick hands, hands like feet, are loosely clasped and sunk in between his thighs. Aneita Jean is snuggled so close, her legs disappear under his. Her arms wrap tightly around his right forearm like a spring. A gentle breeze ruffles her dress, a tight striped number with an open lace collar. My grandmother remembers the car rocking a bit as Howard exhaled.

"He leaned over and we kissed."

They kissed. They kissed harder than they ever had, and they kissed at the worst possible moment, because Andrew

Blair was walking up Phoenix Avenue, coming home from work.

He saw them kissing and he stopped in front of the car bumper, stared down giant Howard Walton with the hands like feet, started screaming about indecency and self-respect, and demanded that if they insisted on carrying on like that, they do it inside the house, where the only people they could offend were people already disgusted with their behavior.

As Andrew Blair stomped up the porch and slammed the screen door, Howard turned weakly to Aneita Jean and said, "Will you marry me?" And Aneita Jean laughed, said, "Just ignore my father; he does that all the time." And Howard said, "No, I'm serious. Will you marry me?" And Aneita Jean, overcome by his devotion, gripped his forearm tight through his suit and started to cry.

•

Here now is a picture of Glen Dingle: the worst date my grandmother ever had, and that is saying something.

Glen Dingle was a slow-witted boy from the upper end. By age fifteen, Glen already owned his own car and had plenty of cash for sweets, jukeboxes, and whiskey. He was also in DeMolay, a prestigious boy's club made up of the sons of the few wealthy families in the area. To date a DeMolay boy was considered a prize, even a DeMolay like Glen, "who couldn't count to twenty-one unless he was naked."

They were going to take a drive through the holler, maybe stop and pick daises. Glen was different from Aneita

Jean's other boyfriends in that he was one of the few boys
in the Ohio River valley who was born soft, cushioned
from worry by the muffling security of family money. Even
his hands were smooth, and when Aneita Jean first felt
them, she unconsciously flinched, feeling as if she'd acci-
dentally slipped her fingers into a tub of bacon lard.

Glen liked belonging to DeMolay. He especially liked
the uniform, a white dress shirt, necktie, and snug navy
wool suit strung with silver buttons and cinched just under
the ribs with a thick leather belt. He enjoyed the stiffness of
the cloth, the way other men would nod as he passed them
on the street. That he had done nothing to warrant wearing
a uniform didn't concern him.

Glen was wearing his uniform when he picked up
Aneita Jean, even though it was seventy-five degrees outside
and the wool itched like a mess of chiggers.

"You look like a policeman," she said as she climbed in
his car. "Thank you," said Glen.

They decided to drive straight to the daisy field, which
sat just outside of town. She had been there many times
before with another beau, Earl, a fact she shared with
Glen.

"The last time we were here, Earl made this really long
daisy chain," she said animatedly, leaning toward Glen, one
ankle tucked under her rump. "And he wrapped me up in it
like a mummy! Isn't that a scream?"

Glen let out a little bark of a laugh and adjusted his hat.
She tried again.

"Earl is forever taking pictures of me. Especially"—she
leaned close enough for Glen to feel her breath on his ear—
"from behind."

Glen pulled over, screeching the car to a halt. Aneita

Jean jolted back, her eyes wide. She tried not to smile. Glen exhaled slowly and lugubriously, like a pricked tire under water.

"Jeannie," he said finally. "I'm tired. Do you mind driving?"

Her jaw dropped. She didn't drive. She understood the gist, had absorbed enough to get by from playing with the Nash in the garage with her brother Petey. But girls weren't required to drive. Maybe if someone was dying and the original driver had been thrown from the car and there was no one else for miles and she wouldn't be seen racing to the hospital. Maybe then. But otherwise, girls were meant to be driven.

She eyed Glen in his ridiculous outfit as he exited the car and loped around the grille. She slid over into the driver's seat, briefly considering flooring the gas pedal and leaving him on the roadside to wilt. Glen settled noisily into the passenger's side, shot my grandmother a dispirited look, and, within minutes, fell asleep, his petit head flush with the seat. Aneita Jean sighed, swung the car around, and started toward home, singing loudly.

"I used to be on the daisy chain, but now I'm a dimestore daisy."

When she crossed the Little Blue Bridge into Chester, she grabbed Glen's precious DeMolay cap and sailed it into the river.

Glen, says my grandmother, was a "little nothing." He was not a "something else," like Bill Thorton, who was studying for the priesthood when he met Aneita Jean, and quit soon after. Nor was he a "long-sufferer," like Howard and the others. Grandmother collected long-sufferers. She knew that long-sufferers made the best dates because they were always trying to impress, hopeful that maybe that night would be *the* night, never guessing that the very earnestness they labored to project had killed their chances from the get-go.

"I wasn't interested in love," she says. "I was interested in life."

•

H*ere now is a picture of Orville Smail.*
Orville Smail was a good dancer. He had the moves. And he was rich. Which was good, because Orville Smail was ugly as mud.

Orville, bless his heart, had the face of a creekbed. His cheeks sunk in like divots, as did his eyes. His ears compensated by fanning out as if to catch the sun. His lips were oddly shaped. His head resembled an upturned squash. Matters improved little as you moved downward. Orville, sadly, was built like a pipe cleaner, and his clothes, tailored suits and two-toned shoes, hung off him like moss on a branch.

Orville snapped most of the photographs of my grandmother in the album. The lovely Aneita Jean at the Little Blue Bridge, in the park, propped on wood piling with her dress blown up to her garters. Orville and Aneita Jean laughed a lot when they were together, and Orville noticed how when she laughed, she would reach out to touch his arm or his shoulder and give it a gentle squeeze. Which got him to thinking.

The two had been dating for months. And Orville knew he had done all the right things. He spent money freely, took Aneita Jean on trips in his convertible, told her with gratuitous frequency how beautiful she was. She had met his sister and his mother. And some weekends, they all took road trips together to the Mystic Caverns or Harpers Ferry. He kept a photograph of her from one of these trips on his dresser mirror. In it, she is sitting atop his convertible, legs spread, her mouth open midlaugh, the hood ornament jutting up right between her legs.

Orville knew Aneita Jean saw other men. He also knew most of them were poor, potters and mill workers, and that she would never settle for staying in the valley. That was in his favor.

His plan was to seduce her with music. So one night, at a friend's apartment, he sat her on the couch and produced a recorder. The recorder allowed them to capture their voices on homemade albums. Aneita Jean had never seen anything like it, and she and Orville sat for hours singing songs, hamming, and laughing till they were short of breath. Orville tried to choose lyrics that would melt her heart, and she did seem appreciative, leaning closer as he sang and applauding loudly when he was finished. He dedicated each song to her, puffing up his bony chest and crooning in his best Johnny Mercer voice.

On the drive home, Orville stopped just off Phoenix Avenue and parked the car.

"What are you doing?" Aneita Jean asked. "Is something wrong?"

Orville said nothing, he didn't even move his head while he fumbled in his trouser pocket and pulled out the jewel box. When she saw the box, she fell silent.

"I bought you this ring," he said. And that was all. Aneita Jean took the box and opened it. Inside was a huge sapphire set in silver. She slipped it on her ring finger. It fit.

It was the most expensive thing she had ever touched. She flicked her finger up and down, feeling the weight of it, and thought about a life with Orville. She thought about all the places she would go. She thought about money and the oddity of never having to worry about where it would come from. She looked into Orville's craggy, frail face, and imagined that life.

She wore the ring all the way home, spun it around on her finger, checked its color in the fading light. When they arrived at her house, she took it off and held it one last moment, feeling its heft in her palm.

"I can't," she said.

Orville thrust her hand away and stared out over the car hood.

Aneita Jean opened her door and stepped out, the ring still rattling loose in her hand.

"Keep it," he said in a reedy voice. "In case you come around."

My grandmother did not come around, but she still has the ring.

•

H*ere now is a picture of Don Thornberry.*
    "I called him 'Tyrone Gable,' " she says.

Edna called him "Sir Don."

His own mother called him by his given name, Donald Leslie, or sometimes "idiot."

Donald Thornberry never wanted to be anybody until he saw Aneita Jean Blair, and then he wanted to be the man Aneita Jean Blair married.

It was never a decision. It just was. He was a boy in love with a girl, and that was that. What to do next was a problem. He knew she knew. He figured everybody knew. His feelings were loud as plaid, his desperation flagrant. Sometimes, he felt like his bones were sticking through his skin. His stomach hurt all the time. He would have done anything to meet her. As it turned out, nothing needed to be done. Their fates were set to collide. That was the beauty of a small town. Everybody collided at one point or another. People said it was God, but it was really just geography.

He first saw her one day when they were both twelve years old, up the road from Newell, as he was walking the streets of Chester, where the houses had yards and wraparound porches and enough space in between that you didn't hear your neighbor's toilet flush.

He had just turned down Phoenix Avenue and was waiting by the trolley stop when he heard it.

"My bonny lies over the ocean," the voice sang, amid giggles and the tortured squeal of a ukulele. "My bonny lies over the sea."

He moved closer, past the trolley stop, to the edge of the yard. He squinted and cocked his head like a dog.

"My bonny lies over the ocean."

He walked onto the yard, past the porch, clear to the window, and there was Aneita Jean, wriggling and giggling in the living room, sitting atop the braided rug, belting out a tune and snapping her ukulele while a group of her daddy's friends from the factory sat rapt, clapping a bit harder than they should.

Don watched her there with the men inside, and he fell over with laughter.

My grandmother saw him through the window, some Newellie boy in neat clothes shuddering on her front stoop, slapping his thigh, darn near crying from it all, and she rolled her eyes and kept right on singing and strumming, and by the time she shot a second annoyed glance back to the window, the Newellie boy was gone.

Don Thornberry

Donald Leslie Thornberry was the eldest son of Alvin and Erla Thornberry. Alvin was a potter, and he had been since he was old enough to spit. He was born in 1893, at a time when his father had to half-sole his shoes and birthday presents took the form of whittled sticks.

Alvin was one of seven kids born to Minnie and Frank. His people were colorful. He had an aunt who danced a Russian jig in special furry boots, and an uncle who ran a hotel in East Palestine, Ohio. For entertainment, they hunted hickory nuts in the hollers, roasting them later over trash fires.

When the family moved to Newell, houses were scarce and people kept hogs in their backyards. The roads were made of scraped dirt. There was no school or local church. School classes were held in a room above the post office.

Before the move, Alvin and his siblings had attended classes in a one-room schoolhouse with a metal stove in the kitchen area. His teacher was Molly Allison, and she always brought Alvin an orange and a popcorn ball for Christmas. This new school was nothing to shout about, and there were no popcorn balls or oranges, so Alvin quit and started selling newspapers in East Liverpool. He hollered, "Extra! Extra!" just like in the movies, and took home a few nickels for his trouble. This, too, was nothing to shout about, and so at thirteen, he wrangled a job at the potteries.

He was hired on as a sponger, cleaning cups for sixty cents a day, ten cents more than if he sponged for an apprentice turner. Spongers stood between wooden planks stacked with freshly turned ware. Each piece was hand-sponged, the sponge snagging any remnants and brushing them off, smoothing the rough edges. It was women's and children's work—repetitive, with no heavy lifting. Every morning, his mother packed a lunch and he'd ride the nickel trolley to the pottery. After the streetcar fare, Alvin would net fifty cents.

From then on, Alvin's life was pretty well set. At sixteen, he joined the church when Billy Sunday threw up a tent in East Liverpool and called a handful of local boys to choose a faith. Alvin wasn't much for faith, but he was wild for girls, and he knew whichever church he chose would in effect be narrowing his choices for a wife, so he chose to become a Presbyterian.

When he was seventeen, a neighbor bought a radio. It was the first in Newell, and everybody gathered in the yard to listen outside the window. It seemed impossible to him that voices could carry so far. "Begorry!" he said to himself. "We done it now."

Shortly after that, word came of a new pottery opening in Erwin, Tennessee. Better wages, easier winters. Lured by mystery and promises, most of Alvin's family pulled up stakes and left. Along with eight other families, they loaded all their furniture in a railway boxcar and headed south. Alvin stayed behind.

He liked Newell and his job as a sponger. He liked the park and the ball games and the way the West Virginia air wrapped around his gums and vibrated his teeth to the roots, how he could actually feel the cool of it whistle through his throat and travel down to his lungs as if propelled by its own unknown desires. So Alvin stayed, and his family sent him letters and flour sacks full of Blue Ridge chestnuts.

Eventually, Alvin became a turner, then a handler at HLC. He married Erla, a Presbyterian of the most joyless sort, and together they had four children, Vaun, Velma, Donald, and Ernie. In the summer, they'd all ride the running boards of the streetcar to Rock Springs Park and spend the day tossing a ball or making whistles out of grass blades.

The family lived at the end of Grant Street, one block from HLC. The house was two stories high and had three bedrooms, one bath. Don was born in an upstairs bedroom in 1920, while his father was at work sticking handles onto coffee cups and flattening the edges with his thumb.

•

"I broke a lot of dates with Don because he couldn't take me anyplace," my grandmother explains. "He didn't have a car or any money. He'd ride his bike all the way from Newell, and then we would ride together, me on Petey's bike and Don on his. We'd ride around the upper end, which felt like it was clear at the end of the world."

Don Thornberry was earnest, decent, upright. Bled of selfishness and fire by the unique responsibilities of being the eldest boy born to a father who drank.

"Go down to the Legion and fetch your pap!"

Don's mother, Erla, worked at the pottery as a secretary, when she wasn't having babies or at church, praying for her husband's sins. Alvin had always liked his drink. He swilled a nip before work and a good many after. The drink never made him nasty. It only ratcheted up his already-mischievous personality, which was irritation enough to Erla.

She was of English descent and believed this made her more worthy of just about everything. To reinforce her point, she always wore heels and carried a fox stole, the type with the head still attached as a clasp; the hinged jaw with its little razor teeth pinched open and shut on various parts of the animal's torso. Even in the summer, there she'd be, sweltering in the stole, her neck rashy from the heat, the razor teeth digging into the fox's former belly.

"She was a short, mean thing who never gave any love to anybody," Grandmother says. "She was very active in the church."

There is a photograph of Erla and Alvin in the memory book. The two of them are standing side by side in front of Erla's car. (Erla forbade anyone else to drive it, forcing her husband to sit in the back with the kids, where she could more effectively ignore him.) In the photo, Erla has one hand on her hip and the other cupped on Alvin's shoulder. Alvin's arms are crossed, his body leaning reluctantly into his wife's breast. Erla's lips are pursed into a weary half smile. Alvin's lips are wrinkled dramatically in resignation.

Can you believe my rotten luck? Erla seems to ask.

Can you believe mine? Alvin's expression counters.

Their eldest daughter, Vaun, was a sour girl whose face tugged down at the corners. Smiles pained her, so she generally didn't bother. She steeped in her misery until her suspicions were confirmed, first by her mother—"It's a horrible life, girl. You may as well know it now"—then by experience.

Years later, when her husband, a gruff, pockmarked jiggerman quick with a slap, abandoned her after the birth of their disabled son, Vaun wasn't surprised. Misery was her lot, and she had always known that. "I told you so," her mother said. And she had.

Vaun's younger sister, Velma, tried to make up the difference. She was gentle, quiet, and warm, and she stayed so even after her own husband, Paul, an HLC salesman, turned out to be an alcoholic, a man who came and went as his finances demanded. Often ill, Velma received gold treatments, injections of metal into her blood, which in time crippled her, then killed her in her thirties. When she was sick, Don took care of her. Her mother couldn't be bothered, believing the girl had somehow brought it on herself.

After Don came Ernie, another boy and another drunk.

"Go down to the Legion and fetch your brother!"

Even as young as thirteen, Ernie would toss back whiskey with his father, both laughing like hyenas at the seriousness of big brother Don. Later, when Don took Ernie in, Ernie's envy bloomed to full-on hate, and he began stealing from Don. Don knew, but he never said a word. He never blamed Ernie for anything. Not even after that day in the park when Ernie hit him in the head with a baseball bat, sending him into a fit of dazzling pain and leaving him partially deaf, and giving a lot of other people the impression that he was slow.

Like Aneita Jean, Don avoided his house as soon as he was old enough. Unlike Aneita Jean, he loved the valley. He took long walks and played on any team that would have him. He became a crackerjack footballer. He looked like a whippet when he ran, his lean frame eluding tackles and reaching over lines. He got noticed. "Nice run, Don!" And although it made him uncomfortable, it shifted something inside him for the better.

•

As it turns out, Donald Leslie Thornberry would live his whole life on one square block. It wasn't that he didn't care much about the outside world. He was an active letter writer, usually writing to politicians about what they were doing wrong. He read the papers. He visited Florida now and again. He just preferred the world of his block to anything he read about or saw elsewhere. So when he ate fried shrimp, hours fresh from the Florida Gulf, he swore they weren't as tasty as the fried shrimp at the Newell Elks Lodge, which sat a half block from his home. And when he spent time in the army in Alaska, he thought the land was pretty, but nothing like spring in the holler. Home was beauty and goodness and all that was right, and he didn't care to waste time pretending he thought otherwise.

Every night after dinner, he went outside to smoke. He would sit on the porch glider, his skin dirt-dry in the shifty mountain air, and tell stories to the neighborhood kids. He'd build a fiction spontaneously, from the ground up, usually one starring monkeys and elephants and the trouble they found themselves in. The stories were loose and without lessons, and they went over well with his audience, a gaggle of hillbilly boys and girls sitting at his feet in the swirl of his smoke, eyes closed, traveling. He liked stories. He needed the way they emptied his head and made his chest lighter. He liked being heard, even if the voice felt like somebody else's.

Sometimes when he walked the streets alone, he was overcome by the wonder of the valley. It made him ache, the splendor he saw: the glint of the Ohio River, the factories bathed in steely light, the brown-green of the hills, the sharp gray of the rocks. He loved West Virginia, and he promised himself that he would never abandon her.

This is what he was thinking when he saw twelve-year-old Aneita Jean squealing and singing inside that giant house on Phoenix Avenue. This is what he was thinking when he was twelve years old and just growing into his shoes. This is what he was thinking when he fell in love.

a Alice Blair

CHAPTER ELEVEN

*Let thy son be an intellectual giant and a skillful
workman if he may, but by all means let him be a
skillful workman.*

—FROM *THE WEST VIRGINIA
BOOK OF HARANGUES*

When you work at the pottery or the mill or the mine, you come to understand certain truths. Hands are lopped off. Bones are broken. Machines grind men up. Mines collapse. Lungs clog. Men drink. Women gossip. You are born knowing that most people get lost, that their stories die with them. You expect little else. And so you talk a lot about nothing and you get shit-faced and you welcome violence if for no other reason than because you can ignite it.

Those who can stop themselves from thinking too much do so. They fill the hours in other ways. In Hancock County, Thelma sabotaged Velma's pie in the pottery bake-off. Reverend Haddock used church funds to buy booze from Broomhall's grocery. Mr. Broomhall placed the Reverend Haddock's bets at the bookie's. Husbands cheated, wives wept, everyone gambled, and everyone lied about what they lost. Magic, any specter of a miracle, was what mattered to the people of the valley. That and stubborn faith. Mysteries made life bearable, and more often than not, they were kissed up to God with a shrug and a slug of whiskey. And if folks went screaming mad, shouting at the rain or soaring plates into the holler or talking to Jesus Christ Almighty, no one assumed they'd been dropped on their heads. (During one six-week revival in Newell in 1912, there were six thousand recorded religious conversions.)

All of this slid into my grandmother's consciousness easy as a snake into water. When it came to the truth, my grandmother possessed a natural instinct for avoidance, which served her well in Hancock County, where thinking just gave people ideas, and ideas put a real dent in productivity.

Reality was never her concern.

"I was going to be Bette Davis," she says matter-of-factly.

In her tenth-grade class photo, my grandmother is standing in the back row, dead in the center, in a starched pinstripe button down and a striped tie. She is taller than her classmates, an effect exacerbated by her hair, which is curly and wild, like a nest woven of red silk thread. Her eyes are playful. She is standing ramrod-straight.

The girls around her are an irresolute lot. All are wearing puritanical dresses, heavy, shapeless black frocks adorned with frills and crosses. Most are slumping, curled at the shoulders, desperately trying to shrink themselves and melt away into their funereal shifts. They look almost damp, and it is clear from their eyes that none have any idea about leaving West Virginia. And while they probably do have an idea about Bette Davis, they sure as shit aren't going to believe for one second that they could be like her.

"They all thought I looked ridiculous," she says of her classmates. "Ah, so what if I did."

Each year, her body grew more and more liquid. She grew taller. Her breasts became more impertinent. Her belly settled into a soft curve. More than ever, she could feel the hunger of men when she walked down the street, the weight of their stares on her thighs. And she would swing her hips a little wider, throw her shoulders back, drop the occasional pencil.

Her seductions were limitless.

There were Happy Metro and Jackson Reeves and Butch Hillock and Harry McElivy and Marty Flannery and Patches O'Brien and Jock McCoy and Duke and Daniel O'Hara. So many boys coming on and off her front porch, bringing gifts for her mother and wearing their best shirts, rolling the sleeves to hide the stains. She chose ugly men (Orville Smail) and beautiful men (Carl Smith). Stupid men (Glen Ringle) and fat men who dressed well (Benny the Jew). Men with buck teeth (Earl Coe). Men with slick hair (Juney McHenry). Brothers (Jack and Jim Bailey). Old (Cyril Taylor), young (Percy Willis), drunk (Arnett Booker), principled (Don Thornberry), and unscrupulous (John Wilson). All of them wanting nothing more than an hour alone with her, to make her laugh, to smell her neck, to watch as she hitched up her socks and ran her fingernail over her chalky thighs, all imagining a day when the hour would never end.

"Don't forget I'm not long for this place," she'd tell them all.

"Don't, Jeannie. Please don't."

"Ah, horseshit feathers."

To the boys, love was about sandwiches with the crusts cut off and children and a little comfort when you came home from your shift. Or they thought it was, until they met Aneita Jean and she wrecked their worlds with whispers of another.

She liked these boys because her effect was measurable, perceptible. Because she knew when she was with them, and their breath quickened and their pants rose and their skin went clammy, that she existed, that she was real. She was not, as she was at home, an insect unnoticed until it made a sound. She was not, as she felt alone in her room, an apparition, carved out and mowed smooth by the massage of unwelcome hands.

While her girlfriends were frantically honing in on potential lifelong mates, Aneita Jean spun the revolving door off its hinges. She saw marriage as an endless chore, an erosion of will, a heaving capitulation. Marriage was a shrug. She had long ago decided that the dutiful girlfriend becomes the dutiful wife. And with that realization, she had given in entirely to her shallowest instincts and run whole hog into the bliss of debauchery.

•

Aand then the war came.
Not right away, but the signs were there, news from overseas pricking dread under the bone. By 1938, pottery supplies were already being rationed. The use of zinc oxide, borax, and paper cartons was curtailed, the limitations ushering in whole crises of pottery reformulation and packing standards. Details about such changes took up many columns of the "Pottery News."

By then, the Depression had culled the potteries so much that only a few major factories remained. HLC, Harker, and Hall eked by, while the rest folded, laying off hundreds of men and women. To spur commerce, there was no charge for public transportation, and signs were erected, urging people to support the local industry: SHOP IN THE POTTERY CENTER OF THE WORLD. Of course, nothing would help until the war proper, when boycotts of Japanese dishware and the removal of aluminum, steel, and iron from general circulation would revive the demand for china and earthenware. But this was all in the future, unknown, unanticipated, and in the interim, folks slogged along, uncertain and trapped within their skins.

In the years leading up to the war, the Homer Laughlin China Company introduced what would become their most successful product of all time: Called Fiesta Ware, it featured bowls and plates with incised rings. The colors were optimistic: cheery red, sunny yellow, splashy green, sudsy ivory, and dark blue. Turquoise was added later. The line had an unprecedented look—bold and comfortable. The word *casual* was even stamped on the bottom. A 1938 advertisement for the line read "Now the parade of color invades the kitchen too!"

HLC was making a conscious effort to lift the country's spirits. How could you be depressed in a kitchen filled with china that was "brilliant and eye-catching"?

"Emphasis is withdrawn from the drab . . . and placed heavily upon brightness, gaiety, color!" chirped the Fiesta brochure. "It's FUN to set a table with Fiesta!"

In 1939, a 109-piece set sold for $14.95, and the line became, in the terms of the day, "a vogue." Fiesta was synonymous with young America. A poster from the American Dairy Council even showed foods resting on Fiesta plates:

> *I sit up straight and tall you see*
> *It's most important all agree*
> *To look your best and feel that way*
> *That's why I eat well every day.*

By 1940, the line had expanded to incorporate everything from condiment jars to cake servers. With no kitchen need unaddressed (they even made single-olive serving trays), HLC began firing miniature animals—fish, penguins, ducks, lambs, cats, turtles, and donkeys. The animals were collected and widely imitated by other potteries. The donkey became the outsize favorite, as a 1940 HLC newsletter proudly states, "far out-selling any of the other animals in the line."

Absurdity, the proud essence of West Virginia, had become a national refuge. A war was beckoning, and Americans were all googly over a prancing green ass.

"It was the waiting," says grandmother. "It made us all crazy."

Many unemployed potters looked for work at the sawmill or the steelworks. Those who didn't enlist in the armed services tried the brickyard, or left Hancock County altogether, hoping their luck would be better someplace else. The rest drank in Steubenville, Ohio, or on their porches, slugging back homemade liquor that took a layer of throat with it.

The juke joints in Steubenville served warm Coke and bourbon in plastic cups. The results weren't good. It felt like drinking a glass of fur. Nobody cared, because the music was free. It was outside of Ollie's, in the gravel parking lot, that Frank Walton first pummeled Don Thornberry.

It started the night before. Don, a seventeen-year-old high school junior, had made the key run in the football game, getting the snot knocked out of him as he was yanked down. As soon as he staggered up, he looked for his Jeannie and saw her standing in the second row, hand over her mouth, afraid, and he jumped to his feet and bobbed his head to let her know he was okay. Aneita Jean knew Don was in love with her. She could tell because he looked at her like an animal in need of a feed.

After the game, they met on the sidelines and he gave her his sweater, a white one with a big fuzzy green N on the front. She snatched it up and draped it around her shoulders. He walked her home, and because he made the key play in the game, she let him kiss her good night.

"You wearing that?" Edna asked the next morning

when Aneita Jean came downstairs for school, Don's Newell letter sweater tucked tightly into a pair of wide-legged trousers.

"I don't see why not," she answered.

"You're asking for trouble, Jeannie. You know Newell and Chester are rivals."

"Doesn't mean anything to me." And it didn't really. Not when she heard whispering behind her in the halls. Or when her other Chester boyfriends got red-faced and panicky. Or when she was finally sent home for refusing to take the sweater off. It was disrupting class, causing a stir, which, as far as she could gather, was what sweaters were meant to do in the first place.

"Happy now?" Edna asked when she walked back in the door an hour after leaving.

She was. But she didn't say so.

•

Frank and Don only fought for three minutes. Don was quick and Frank was drunk, so it was short work all around. It was different the night with Howard Anderson. Anderson was twice Don's size and smart enough to fight sober. Don knew it was coming. Howard had said so earlier in the day, but Don knew well before that. He knew because Howard was in love with Jeannie, just like he was in love with Jeannie, and all of them, these stymied, frustrated lovers of Aneita Jean Blair, well, all of them fought eventually.

"I'm going to get you, dingleberry," snarled Howard.

Don said nothing, just kept walking at a steady pace.

After school, Don headed home, passing HLC, Sixth

Street and the town's only traffic light, and then the post office. As he strolled by the empty lot across from the barbershop, Howard fell in step beside him, and Don knew it was time. Howard faced him right and honorable, the first punches landing thick, like stacked wood. Aneita Jean came to watch. She didn't root for either man, nor did she ask them to stop. She just stood silently on the side of the lot and watched as they flung and sweat, spit knocking out of their mouths, knuckles popping open, lips splitting, then puckering like overripe peaches.

When it was over, the two men limped to the Washington Club for a shot of bourbon and Coke. Aneita Jean patted their foreheads with a napkin.

"Don's the only man in the group," said Howard, raising his cup as she dabbed at his cuts, his left eye jiggly and loose, like an egg cracked in a pool of flour.

He and Don clinked their drinks and chugged them back.

"Who wants to dance?" Aneita Jean asked.

•

Aneita Jean had met Don not long after he spied her singing in her living room window on Phoenix Avenue. It was on the Fourth of July, at Rock Springs Park. They were both thirteen years old.

On the day they met, she was wearing her mother's shoes, tie oxfords with a heel, and a loose dress. She and Snook had gone to the park to watch the fireworks. It was an inauspicious day, common and hot, and there was no indication in the air, no tremors or music or piercing light, that this would be the day that would change her life forever, because if there had been, she certainly would have worn something sexier than her mother's shoes.

Since that day on Phoenix Avenue, Donald Thornberry had made it his business to spot Aneita Jean as often as possible. When he could, he would ride to Chester on his brother's bike and coast slowly past her house, so slowly that he might have toppled over. On the night of the fireworks, he'd borrowed his father's dress pants and a long-sleeved dress shirt. He'd even slicked some pomade in his curly black hair.

"I'm Donald Thornberry," he said, extending his hand like his mother had taught him.

"So?" Aneita Jean said, smiling at Snook, who giggled and looked at the ground.

"What's your name?"

"Jeannie Blair. What's yours?"

"Donald Thornberry. I just told you."

"So you did."

Then Donald introduced his friend Kenny Klein, Aneita Jean introduced Snook, and the fireworks began.

Don tried to watch, but his eyes kept wandering to Aneita Jean's face, her eyes popping wide with each explosion. She knew he was watching, so she concentrated on keeping her face soft, like she'd seen Jean Harlow do in the pictures. She noticed him smiling a little. She noticed something else, too. Donald Thornberry from Newell was handsome.

Donald Thornberry was tall and thin, like her father, with biceps as big as canned hams. Huge, bulbous muscles balled up high in his arms, as if they'd been crammed there with a boot heel, forcing him to wear his shirtsleeves rolled well past his elbows, almost to his shoulders. His trousers were hitched up by braces and cuffed just past the ankle, giving them a gentle break in the leg. His shoes were spit-polished and effulgent as burnished chrome. And he smelled clean. Like he'd given himself a rough scrubbing, which he had.

When the fireworks ended, Aneita Jean suggested the four of them take a stroll around lover's lane.

"I can't," said Snook, again giggling and looking at the ground.

"Me, neither," said Kenny.

"Looks like it's just you and me, Don," she said with a wink.

And Don, insides thick and quivery, gave his best firm nod, took Aneita Jean's arm, and led them both into the woods.

'Pete'

CHAPTER TWELVE

The spring in Newell never loses its chill. Even on the warmest days, the breeze moves the heat around, so the cold still hits you in patches, like a tossed bucket of water. The day Petey Dink went hunting with his best friend, George Kelly, was especially soggy and dank. A week of rain had ushered in decay, and the smell of it hung in the woods like a tent.

Both boys had graduated from high school and had decided to go shooting in the holler to celebrate. Edna packed them off with a lemon cake. George brought the whiskey.

On the hike in, they talked about the pottery. George wanted to haul ware. He liked the idea of loading up crates and taking them out of town, driving through the mountains to make deliveries, then coming back on the weekends to hunt with his hounds.

They talked and they drank. And then, bored, they began chasing each other. George pushed Petey over and ran past him, teasing him.

"You! Big! Pussy!"

Petey picked himself up and gave chase, the two of them running pell-mell, sloshing through cricks, their pants sticking fast to their shins. Pete caught George after about a half a mile and tackled him to the ground, the two of them rolling over and over, leaves stuck in their sodden hair, their bellies rigid with laughter and cold.

"Who's the pussy now, big guy?"

No one remembers how George's gun went off. But it did. One shot. In the chest.

Aneita Jean was walking home from the store when she saw George sitting on the front porch, paper white and wild-eyed. She had never seen him look scared. She instantly felt sick.

Petey.

She ran past George and went into the house, where the doctor and her mother and father were circled around the couch.

Pete was stretched out on top. He was alive, but laid low and wheezing.

"Hey there, Jeannie," he said, reaching out his fingertips.

"Be still, boy," his father snapped. Then he added quietly, "Be still, for God's sake."

Edna hugged her daughter as the four of them listened to the doctor explain why he couldn't remove the bullet. They nodded blankly, trying to rearrange their facial features into something resembling calm. Either Pete's body would plug up and fight or it would resent the intrusion and swell with infection.

"I'm sorry I can't be of more help," said the doctor.

"Yes, yes, of course." They nodded, adhering to politeness as the air bled from their lungs. "Thank you ever so much," they said, when what they really wanted was to strangle the doctor and leave him to rot on the highway.

Aneita Jean ran back outside to the porch. She stared at George, looked him right in the eye. Minutes ticked by. He did not look away.

"It was an accident," he said, gulping air. "It was an accident."

Aneita Jean kept staring, staring, staring until George looked down at his pants, which were stained with blood and sweat. He started to shake. She watched him there for a minute, then took his shivering hand in hers. George began to sob. They sat like that for a good while.

•

Pete survived the bullet. And George Kelly never touched Aneita Jean again. In fact, within a month, he moved away from the valley and tried to make a go as a road musician, playing trumpet in juke joints in exchange for drinks.

He would come back a couple of years later, when the

war had changed everything, and take a job hauling ware in
the pottery, which turned out to be harder and lonelier than
he'd imagined. When he would see Aneita Jean, he would
wave and smile politely, giving no indication of all those
nights they had spent together, he lying on her body, stealing her girlhood like penny gum, then washing his hands
after, leaving her dirty.

When he waved, Aneita Jean simply waved back, as if
nothing extraordinary had ever passed between them.

·

After Pete got shot, Don Thornberry gained some
ground. He was the only boy to come around with a
fruit basket. Fruit he had to work double shifts at the pottery after school to pay for. Fruit he walked with all the way
from Newell, the basket held in front of him like a platter,
the handle too small to fit over his shoulder. This gesture
impressed both Edna and Andrew, Edna because it was
sweet, Andrew because it was labor-intensive.

Petey Dink was a fan of Don's. He thought Don was a
bit serious for a seventeen-year-old, but as the two of them
spent hours talking while Pete recovered on the sofa, Pete
decided Don was all right, and he told his sister as much.

"Don't mess with that one, Jeannie," he chided her.
"He doesn't deserve it. If you had any brains at all, you'd
marry him."

Nineteen, out of school and working at the pottery,
Petey Dink was of the marrying age, and he thought his sister should realize that she was, too.

"Playing the field is good when you're a kid, Jeannie.
But you don't want to wait too long."

Aneita Jean considered these opinions, but there were problems. Don wasn't going anywhere. He was a hoopie, and he didn't even care. He was sweet, but he didn't own a car or have any cash. Worst of all, he didn't have "it." No ambition, no crude sexuality, no vein of cruelty running through him like a fissure through marble. Clear thinking was not Aneita Jean's forte to begin with, and so she saw Don, but she continued to see Howard and Earl and Dick Pugh, and, when they grew dull, Charles and Harry and a few others. Boys Petey called "good-for-nothings," but boys who had, in varying quantities, "it," the smallest dose of which could turn even the smartest girl into a soggy mess of bad instincts.

"I like them big," Aneita Jean explained when Snook asked what she saw in some of her beaux.

"What about all the rest?" Snook asked, knowing full well that many of her friend's suitors were not only small but also failures on all counts.

"Beats sitting home, don't you think?" Aneita Jean would answer.

Which explains Percy Willis.

Percy was a hoopie, an unpopular kid with flat hair and a sunken chest, a sad-mugged fellow with the kind of loose-fleshed body that looked as if you could pick any spot and push your finger straight through to the bone. He was also cursed with a strangely large head. When he touched it with his small hands, they resembled spiders on a water-melon. The upper-enders tormented him ruthlessly, spitting from their cars or snatching up his underwear in the school hallway.

"You're going to the shed, Percy," said one of the boys on a roasting Friday afternoon. "This weekend. Be ready."

Percy knew about the shed. At the pottery, there was a water trough in the center of the cooper shed where the men soaked staves for barrel binding. It stank so badly, you'd walk miles around it. And chances were that he would end up there, just like those upper-enders said.

Aneita Jean was there when they threw him in.

"Take a bath, Percy," they taunted. Then, laughing and jolly, they drove away, leaving Percy awash in stink.

Aneita Jean stayed put.

"I'll tell you what," she said, eyeing Percy and his sticky clothes. "You get cleaned up, and then you and me will go dancing tonight."

Percy didn't believe her.

"You're full of it," he said, wringing out his shirttail, only to have the liquid pool into his trouser cuffs.

"Try me."

And so it was that Percy Willis and Aneita Jean ended up at the Washington Club, swinging in circles, ribs out and eyes ablaze.

•

What Aneita Jean did not expect was that someday, despite the most careful planning, she would fall in love. It was sudden and sickening, and it scared her to death.

His name was Carl and he had a square jaw and a high forehead. He was a fair-skinned blond. A German who projected solemn reserve. His one indulgence was the trumpet, which he played wildly. When he blew his horn, he became feral, a jazzman mopping his forehead and tapping his snug shoes in a manic rhythm. This made Carl easy to want, but

there was more. He had honor and pride and carried himself so. He projected an air of disdain, which drew Aneita
Jean like a gnat to a peach.

She saw him that night at the Washington Club, saw
him over Percy's giant head, and just that glimpse of him
made her tremble.

•

Persistent, Don kept calling. He and Aneita Jean would
take walks and sit in her father's garden, picking the
petals off roses. Sometimes he'd take her for rides on his
bicycle handlebars. Fettered and quiet, Don said little,
often bumping into her on their walks, fumbling stiffly
with her hand. Once he brought her a piece of Doublemint
gum.

"He thought that was really great," says Grandmother.

When he did talk, it was usually about the pottery.

"Homer Laughlin's opening another plant just to handle their dime-store business."

"You don't say?"

"Homer Laughlin's introducing a new shape in dinner-
ware."

"Oh, really?"

"They're also working on a nonreflective glaze."

"Ah, horseshit feathers, Don. Do you think we could
just neck for a while?"

•

Don took Aneita Jean home only once when they were
courting. His father, Alvin, was out spending his

wages on booze. His mother was at the church, gossiping and praying with the other pub widows. And so Don and Aneita Jean were alone.

They sat on the sofa, hip-to-hip, looking into the living room and saying little. Don was not taught to charm. His pappy knew charm; he had to, so that he'd be let back in the house. His brother, Ernie, had less charm than his pappy, which was unfortunate, because he drank more. Erla saw to it that her eldest boy had no time for charm, or liquor, either, and while it made him a respectable, solid man, it left him thunderstruck when it came to sitting hip-to-hip on the couch with a girl in the fade of the day.

And so they sat in silence, the two of them. Sat there until the sun dipped behind the mountains and the room grew dark, and then the door opened.

Alvin stumbled through, rammed his knee on the sofa, and swore. He hopped around a bit, slurring to himself, failing to notice his son and his son's date, the pretty red-head with the wide eyes. He waddled to the corner of the room, unzipped his pants, and began the slow, laborious release of the night's whiskey onto the family radio.

Aneita Jean wanted to laugh. She didn't know what else to do. Toilet matters in her house were strictly confidential, never spoken of, let alone seen. Her own father would sooner lose an arm than urinate in public. And here was Don's daddy, bare-assed and listing, making a puddle big enough to fill a bucket.

But she held her laughter in, because when she stole a glance at Don, his jaw was set so hard, it inflated the veins in his neck.

Alvin finished, left his fly unzipped, and tripped into the

kitchen, where he began to sing, "She was only a farmer's daughter, but all the horse men knew her."

It proved too much for Aneita Jean. The giggles leaked out staccato-style, until she was nearly hyperventilating. Don stayed silent, his eyes a wash of humiliation. He took Aneita Jean's hand and led her out the door. He said nothing as they rode the trolley back to Chester. And he said nothing when he dropped her off at Phoenix Avenue. He rode home, hearing only the sound of the trolley as it hit the rail supports, *thunk, thunk, thunk,* like doors slamming shut.

CHAPTER THIRTEEN

By 1938, all the Hancock County boys had enlisted or were talking about enlisting, boasting about what they would do if they ever met Hitler. Petey Dink was dejected because his heart condition made him ineligible. He was classified 4-F, and it was the first time in his life that he had ever encountered any resistance to his considerable desires.

His purposelessness sent him deeper into thoughts of marriage, and so, also for the first time, he cut his harem free and kept dating only one woman, Aggie Kimble, a pale, thin girl with narrow brows and a dimple in her chin.

Aggie didn't jump trains or smoke, and she recognized

that Peter Blair would never marry a woman who did. Instead, she gently chided and sighed, kept her hair tidy, and, when necessary, swatted Pete's hands away. When Pete asked Aggie to go steady, she was not surprised.

Aneita Jean had turned eighteen, graduated from high school, and started working for the National Church Supply, a two-story brick factory that manufactured envelopes for church donations. She spent her shift stuffing boxes with crisp new envelopes. It wasn't a glitzy job, but it wasn't the pottery, either. She took the position to save money for college and to help her family with expenses. The wage she earned added enough so that the Blairs could buy bananas and the daily paper.

Her uncle Ralph had lost his job and moved into the house. One day, he just materialized in his overalls, his hair thinning, and Andrew was too despondent to throw him out.

Ralph took a part-time job hauling ware, but he drank too much, so little hauling got done. Aneita Jean would wake early and make orange juice with shaved ice because Ralph liked his juice extra cold. Then she would wipe down the kitchen, make breakfast for her siblings, and walk to work in the morning crisp. She'd work until dinnertime, putting down her wages at week's end to pay off uncle Ralph's hauling truck and the other family debts. Forbie had already joined the navy. Alan helped some by getting an after-school job at the mill firing furnaces, but soon he, too, left to train as a flier for the navy. In his absence, it fell to Aneita Jean to keep the family afloat.

•

Almost as soon as Aneita Jean decided she was in love with Carl, she also decided that he must never know. So she took digs at his character, pulling faces behind his back, talking to herself about his obvious deficiencies. One, he was pious. Always blowing his trumpet in church on Sunday like he thought he was a real musician or something. It was church. You couldn't have found a less discriminating audience if you'd tried.

And then there was that day he took her to his father's farm.

"When I get married, all this will be my wife's," he said, sweeping his arm over the landscape as if serving a tray of sandwiches.

"All what? Who wants to work on a farm in West Virginia for all eternity?"

"Nothing wrong with West Virginia, Jean. Farming, either."

"Well, I don't plan on staying here much longer."

"No one is asking you to, Jean."

In reality, Aneita Jean would have gone to prison if it meant being with Carl, and Carl, for his part, was bright enough to know it.

The two dated, but Aneita Jean made sure she saw Carl only as much as any other man. Not that it mattered. When she did see him, she felt crippled and weak. When he kissed her hello on the cheek, her body tingled, caterpillars crawling on her backbone. He wasn't eager like the other boys. Aneita Jean found his ambivalence more arousing than any hand-delivered bouquet. Sometimes she would carve his name in the dirt by the river, then wipe over it with her foot.

The threat of war had brought everything in Hancock County close to the skin. Laughter was laced with urgency.

Lust shot through everyone's veins. West Virginia, like all of America, was living close to the bone, breathless with trepidation and hungover from apprehension. It was as if a giant finger were tickling down the nation's spine.

Aneita Jean became an expert worrier, her head consumed with minutiae less frightening than the Nazis in Poland. She worried about rain. She worried about money. She worried about who would love her. She worried about slipping on rocks and breaking her arm. She worried that her sweater would unbutton without her knowing it. She worried that her mother would die, that her hair would go flat, that she would never leave West Virginia. She worried all the time, so much so that worry became a constant hum in her brain, an engine running, which she never noticed unless it stopped.

And it did stop. When she was riding in Carl's car and he was telling her she was beautiful and the air was whipping through her clothes, tickling her skin alive. "Drive faster!" she would scream, and Carl would, the tires rubbing a bit on the shoulder gravel, giving the illusion that at any second they might spin out of control and topple headfirst into the valley, immortalized forever in a splintery, fiery heap.

It was then that the humming ceased and Aneita Jean felt the dizzying brain fever of the present, the joy that comes from teetering on the edge, from being slightly mad, from wind through your clothes and burning tires and fear that you open the door for.

•

They heard first from Mrs. Gotchel.

"I see a dark cloud over your house," she told

Edna tersely, waving her hand in the sky as if to scatter smoke.

"What else?" Edna asked.

"That is all I will say."

Edna waited a beat, dropped her nickel, then gathered her skirt, took her daughter's hand, and strode down the street. Once home, Edna went back to work cooking, slicing tomatoes and yams so fast that the chunks would snap from the knife and fall to the floor. She was silent. Her face had become a mask of chalk. Aneita Jean couldn't watch, so she went outside and ran to the river, walking along the banks until dark.

The day it happened, there was a carnival at Rock Springs Park. Hundreds of potters turned out to toss baseballs at bottles and nibble on cotton candy. The air smelled like clean laundry and promise. It was the first cool of the fall. People turned out in their light sweaters and caps, and everyone was in an optimistic mood. Men in newly fitted uniforms winked at girls and walked as if their legs were stuffed with coiled springs. Women flipped their hair like boat sails and smiled with a new ease. It felt as if an invisible belt had been unnotched and all of Hancock County could finally exhale.

The merry-go-round was running. Free ice cream was available for the kids. The pool was also open, and just as the local newspaper had predicted, a large turnout was taking advantage of the last swim of the season.

Petey Dink was having a dip when Aggie showed up. She knelt down by the side, her skirt lifting just past the knee. Petey swam over and peered up into the black between her thighs.

"Peter Blair, I am not impressed," Aggie scolded,

clutching her skirt tightly around her knees. "You should be punished."

"Should I now?" he joked, his green eyes twinkling. Aggie rolled her eyes and then he was off, swimming madly across the pool to the deep end, his arms working like windmills, his legs churning up froth.

He tagged the wall, grinned at Aggie, and headed back as quickly as he'd left, thrashing at the water.

Aggie sat down at the pool's edge. She knew he would kiss her when he reached the shallows. So she sat and waited.

Petey Dink made it back to her side in record time. But something was wrong. His face had turned gray as asphalt and he wasn't smiling. His mouth was snarled up and his eyes were cloudy as dishwater.

"What's wrong?" Aggie said, reaching for his hand.

"Ah, nothing, I'm sure," he said. "Just a little tired." And he put his wet head in her waiting lap and died.

He was twenty years old.

Aggie began screaming. People heard and ran to her side. Men grabbed Petey and shook his shoulders, smacked him on the back. Women turned their children away and wept. Eighteen-year-old Aneita Jean watched in silent horror as her brother died. She didn't know at first. He seemed so content in Aggie's lap. She thought he was resting, that any minute he would vault back into the pool, splashing them all. Aggie would reprimand him for misbehaving. And everything would be as it always had been.

CHAPTER FOURTEEN

When the person you love most dies, you stop believing in much. You pull the shades. You sit very, very still. Your faith floods out, replaced by an overwhelming certainty that all your ugliest thoughts are cast-iron truths.

You ache. And it doesn't stop; it just gets familiar, like walking with a limp.

"There are things people aren't meant to survive," says Grandmother. "I believe that, don't you?"

After Petey's death, the air at 917 Phoenix Avenue became heavy as syrup. Just walking through the house required lurching effort. Nobody talked about his death. It would have been like shaving off a layer of skin.

Andrew Blair disappeared into his studio and sat there making nothing, his features set hard, as if by kiln heat. He stopped talking. The only noise he made was when he rang the studio bell for his supper.

Edna stopped laughing. She sat inside in a windowless corner of the living room, looking into the middle distance. The switch that had flooded her face with light had been flipped off.

Forbes committed himself to his navy training, his letters home brief and few. Alan sent his high school football team to the state championship, tackling the opposition with uncontrolled ferocity. Twelve-year-old Nancy didn't understand the fresh poison in her house, so she stayed away, playing next door from dawn to dusk.

Aneita Jean dated. She didn't know what else to do. Boys asked her out and she went. They still brought chocolates and murmured compliments, but she found that they affected her less. She sat unmoved as they kissed her mouth and felt under her blouse. Her father didn't bother whipping her anymore. No one cared what she did or where she was. Least of all her.

•

The year Petey died, HLC signed up to be part of the 1939 World's Fair, which ran from May through October. The theme was "World of Tomorrow," and HLC made specialty ashtrays and plates to sell, as well as constructing an entire faux pottery that showed viewers every step of pottery production and the people involved, "from slip-maker to the salesman." The exhibit occupied 2,400 square feet and billed itself as "an example of capital and labor working together hand-in-hand." This theme was underscored by a tent-size mural depicting potters going about their business of glaze dipping and kiln loading beneath the floating likeness of W. E. Wells's head.

All the local potters were invited to attend the fair. For just $16.50, they could take the HLC excursion train to New York City, eat a complimentary lunch, and receive two tickets to the exhibit.

The Blairs didn't go.

> *Two little blackbirds sitting on a hill*
> *One named Jack, one named Jill*
> *Fly away Jack, fly away Jill*
> *Come back Jack, come back Jill.*

"We'd play that game all the time, Pete and I," Grandmother says. "It's not much of a game, but we loved it."

And she begins to sob, sixty-four years later.

WILSON   CORP. STANLEY

CHAPTER FIFTEEN

On November 14, 1940, the Chester Purple and Gold played the Newell Big Green. The football game was front-page news on the *East Liverpool Review* sports page, where it was breathlessly announced that the "two teams, famous for their keen rivalry, seem to specialize in shooting the works in this over-important tussle."

Many of the boys would be playing for the last time,

swapping one uniform for another. Even though the draft required only four Hancock County men, Donald Thornberry, Howard Anderson, Carl Law, Earl Coe, Dick Pugh, Harry McHenry, Glen Ringle, Howard Cochran, George Kelly, Charles Taylor, and the Blair boys had already kissed their mothers good-bye and left the valley.

Aneita Jean sent each of them off with a snapshot of herself looking wistfully across the water atop the Little Blue Bridge. In the photograph, she is sitting half-hipped on the wooden railing, her right foot wrapped behind her left calf, her hands clasped loosely in her lap. The wind is blowing her hair and the outline of her camisole is visible beneath her snug V-necked sweater. Her skin is so white, it's almost translucent, contrasting starkly with the pool of black shadow beneath her skirt. She appears empty, indifferent to all the eyes that would be gazing upon her image, the grubby, worn fingers pinching the edges, the bits of tape that would be stuck to corners to adhere her plaintive face to mirrors as far away as Guam.

Food was already being rationed—pork and pork lard, self-rising flour, cornmeal, raisins, eggs, dried prunes. The list changed every month. Aneita Jean noticed how the war brought out strange things in men. The letters she got from boot camps were soft and full of promises, not at all like the sort of thing she used to hear in the backseats on the back roads of the valley. The boastful dreaming had shrunken to simple want.

"Suddenly, they all wanted a family; they all wanted to belong to something."

Aneita Jean didn't feel she belonged to anything. Not anymore. Which is why she figured what she did with Cyril Taylor was okay.

She had met Cyril at the National Church Supply factory. Cyril was British, and he managed the factory where my grandmother spent her days running machines and stuffing boxes full of donation envelopes. She was paid per box stuffed. Cyril was old and married and, most importantly, a painter. He had an easel and canvases and a full set of brushes. "A real artist," she would say to her friends, who wondered why she'd spend any time with a white-haired, bespectacled fifty-year-old man predisposed to wearing woolen vests.

Cyril would prepare lunches for Aneita Jean in his office, usually lobster with homegrown celery that was so crisp, it made a noise when you bit into it, which made her laugh with embarrassment.

They talked about art. Aneita Jean confided she liked the Impressionists because she favored the soft blur of life. Cyril would nod, wipe celery juice from her chin, and offer to show her his techniques. And then she would return to the factory floor to stuff envelopes side by side with the other girls, who envied and adored her in equal measure.

Her best friend at the plant was Roberta Hissom, a stout girl with heavy hair and forearms like a welder's. It was Roberta who took her into the ladies' room and showed her how to smoke.

"You have to drag on it, Jeannie," she said, sucking the butt like a lollipop. "See?"

Aneita Jean dragged, then exhaled slowly, working to control the flow of smoke from her lips. She decided that it made her look sexy, especially the cigarette itself, propped between her dainty fingers, and she determined at that moment that she would smoke as many cigarettes as she could afford.

She and Roberta became fast friends, getting together after hours, taking the trolley to East Liverpool to window-shop.

Aneita Jean made good money at the Church Supply factory, in no small part because of Cyril, who made sure she was assigned the best shifts, operating the cleanest equipment. For her part, she would pack her boxes neatly and leave her lunch hours open.

One day, the company received a brand-new folding machine. Roberta was assigned to man it.

"Jeannie, look!" Roberta said when she first stood behind it. "It's so fast."

Aneita Jean marched straight into Cyril's office.

"I think I deserve a chance on that machine," she said, her voice level.

Cyril swiveled in his desk chair, stood up, and walked to her side. He took her hand and said, "Of course you do, darling."

"But Roberta is my friend," she continued, squeezing Cyril's hand, then dropping it like a rock. "Maybe someone else could decide who should work it."

"What a gorgeous idea, Jeannie," Cyril answered.

Within minutes, Roberta, Aneita Jean, Cyril, and a man from the label division were standing in Cyril's office.

"Now Bob here has seen both you girls work, and I've asked him who he thinks should get to run the folder. Bob?"

Bob looked over Roberta, standing with her feet shoulder width apart, her torso stiff and thick, a Coke in one hand. He then eyed Aneita Jean, who was leaning against Cyril's massive oak desk, her left hip balanced just on the edge.

"Well, Cyril," he said, trying to stifle a grin, "I'm thinking it should be Jean here."

Aneita Jean smiled and clapped her hands, mouthed
"I'm sorry" to Roberta, and rushed out to the floor to
assume her new position. Roberta followed her.

"You know that whole thing was rigged," she said, her
eyes thinned to slits.

"Gosh no," Aneita Jean answered. "I won because I
pack the nicest. You're just jealous."

Roberta rolled her eyes and went out back to smoke.
They never went shopping in East Liverpool again after
that, which turned out to be fine, because Cyril started taking Aneita Jean on road trips to places far more spectacular,
once even meeting her in Pittsburgh.

They were to connect at the train station. Aneita Jean
traveled separately, an arrangement designed to mollify
both her father and Cyril's wife. They reunited at the station. The day was glorious, chilly and cobalt blue, the light
turning the towering buildings to silver. The two went
shopping first. Cyril allowed her to choose a dress and a
pair of shoes for the opera. She tried several outfits, savor-
ing the feel of the satins and crepes as they rippled over her
skin. She settled on a peach satin with a flared skirt and
baby-doll shoulders. For her shoes, she chose orange suede
topped with a tiny rhinestone bow. Taken together, with
her fiery hair and snowy skin, she was, as Cyril proclaimed
many times throughout the night, "a vision."

At the opera, Aneita Jean was overcome by the
sparkling crowd. The men in black tie, the women in layers
of tulle, with long gloves and hair piled high as jasmine,
pinned with jewels. They all sat so perfectly still and
straight. Her father would have approved. Aneita Jean did

her best to look at home, as if she belonged, but it was hard not to swivel her neck and drink in the sea of gorgeousness she'd always known a real city would offer.

Cyril looked only at Aneita Jean. She sensed his eyes on her, and when at one point she was moved to weep, he reached over silently and offered her his handkerchief.

•

Out at base camp in Alaska, the men would snap like twigs. The relentless gray and nut-numbing cold would beat them down, erode their patriotism, leave them weeping in their bunks or bashing their fists into any available surface or jaw. Donald Thornberry was one of the few who went untouched by depression or fury.

In the snapshots he sent from Kodiak in 1941, twenty-one-year-old Don is smiling, his mouth all stretched out, eyes alive and damp, like he'd just landed a prize crappie at the base camp fishing tourney. There are many pictures of him—grinning in front of a mind-bending landscape of ice floe and prairie; firing his pistol into the white; sitting atop a stack of felled logs; sipping from an Old Milwaukee can, his foot resting on a cardboard case.

There are images of him paying hide-and-seek behind a bunker, crouching in front of his cabin (this one says in the margin in blue ink, "Sgt. Don Thornberry Loves You"), and standing cross-armed in front of the mess hall, in front of the whole camp, and in front of a pathetic little clump of haggard trees, many not much taller than he. In the crossed-arm series, he tries to look stern, but he comes off more Gomer Pyle than Patton. In many, his lips twitch up at the corners, like he just can't help himself. And in one, rigged out in full combat gear, he is out-and-out laughing, his mouth wide enough to stick a cat's head in.

"I think he was drunk in that one," says Grandmother.

It's not that Don didn't take his service seriously—he was an intractable patriot—more that he felt goofy being photographed, posing, being made over, and it is a testament to his love for Aneita Jean that he allowed it to happen at all.

He sent the pictures to Chester and they arrived at Phoenix Avenue along with the other pictures from the other servicemen, men looking stoic, or wistful, or miserable as wet dogs. Don was different, solid. He'd endured a hateful mother and an alcoholic father. Boot camp was a square dance by comparison. He felt free there. Free and necessary. He knew his place in the world. And it was a great comfort.

"I found this old mill over the hill," he wrote to Aneita Jean. "And I went panning for gold there, and sure enough here comes this fella with a shotgun and he yells at me, 'What are you doing?' and I say, 'Leaving!' "

"None of those other guys could stand the cold and the dark," says Grandmother. "They would sit around looking at their tent walls. But not Don; he went skiing and hiking. He even went swimming once, said, 'I was in and out so fast, I didn't get wet.' Don could handle it. It's like Howard said: He was the only man in the bunch."

•

The war kept on, and so did Aneita Jean, stuffing envelopes and dating her coterie of men, 4-Fers now, as every able man had gone to war.

"I threw myself to the wolves," she says.

After work, she would meet up with Orville or Benny Phillips, the Jewish racketeer who owned slot machines and could get sugar and butter regardless of rationing.

Once, Benny and Orville showed up on the same night. Aneita Jean was afraid to leave the factory. Her friend Roberta snickered. "Now what, Jean?" They stood side by side, looking out the blinds, as Benny and Orville sat on the street, side by side in their Nash Ambassadors, Benny smoking a cigar, Orville polishing his glasses. Benny was as thick as Orville was thin, his head stumpy and wide as a car battery. Benny stared down Orville, while Orville looked anxiously into the building, where the girls at the factory waited, breathless.

"Come on, Jean, you're gonna have to leave eventually," Roberta said gleefully. "I'm gonna go out there myself if you don't." Aneita Jean stood still. She knew Roberta wasn't going anywhere. She looked hard at Orville, then Benny, and then she grabbed her purse and ran as fast as she could to Benny's car, jumped in, and yelled, "Hurry!"

Benny didn't ask any questions. He just smiled, bit hard on his cigar, and raced down the street. To his credit, Orville followed. And they sped from downtown Chester to the hills, veering left and right through the holler roads, two cars a breath apart, Benny and Aneita Jean laughing in one, Orville gripping the wheel and swearing in the other. They kept at it right through to New Cumberland, Ohio, Benny driving faster and faster until, after cresting a hill, he banked right and skidded to a stop at a double garage hidden in the woods. Orville, as expected, sailed past.

Benny and Aneita Jean usually drove to Steubenville,

where Benny had a buddy who owned a steak house. She loved to go there because Benny seemed to know everybody at the place, and when they walked in, people raised their glasses and shouted, "Hey, big guy," and men with pocket squares would scurry up and kiss her hand while they whispered in Benny's ear.

Benny always encouraged her to eat up, and they'd order the biggest cut of meat, along with potatoes, vegetables, iceberg salad with Italian dressing, and little snips of parsley, which Aneita Jean thought very exotic. When the food came on a huge silver platter, Benny would rub his belly and say, "Now plotz yourself."

When he dropped her home, Benny always had a gift. Sugar, mayonnaise, and butter for her mother. Gas stamps for her father, which Aneita Jean promptly gave to her other boyfriends. Once Benny gave her a rhinestone pin that fanned out on both sides in narrow wings like an angel. She wore it the next time she saw Orville.

Like Benny, Orville was deemed unfit to serve and was therefore left behind to eke out a new brand of masculinity for himself while all the real men were off training to kill Nazis. For Orville, this meant sending back his bacon when it wasn't crisp enough and drinking more than his petit frame could tolerate. One night after Aneita Jean refused his affections, he exploded in a rage.

"Do you know how many girls want to be with me?" he shrieked. "Do you? Do you?"

Knock yourself out, she thought. She was not in a mood for caring. There were so many men drifting in and out of her life, and she found herself weary of making the effort. At home, she saw her mother, fading more every day, never recovering from the loss of Petey Dink, fretful about her other two boys in the navy. In town, Aneita Jean saw her old classmates, married and pregnant, and looking pleased about their choices. She hardly saw her father anymore. It was as if the world had up and left her. It was at these times that she would revisit those photos sent from Alaska. And she remembered the day she first saw Don, laughing at her in the window, and it occurred to her that no other man had ever laughed at her, had ever found her funny.

But he wasn't the one.

•

The most important lesson a woman can teach her daughter is how to be alone. No woman teaches this lesson, of course, as it requires acknowledging that you will be alone. Instead, girls are taught how to love. And they learn the alone part on their own when love fails.

The shrapnel hit Carl's shins and opened them up like a split seam. He was rushed to a hospital, and he sent a letter home asking his family to pray for him. It was shortly after this that he sent Aneita Jean a letter of proposal. He wanted to be wed as soon as he returned from the hospital. He knew they hadn't been together for some time, but he also knew of her love for him, had always known, and he wondered if somewhere in her heart she could still make room for him.

When Aneita Jean received the letter, she wasted no time writing him back.

"Come home," she wrote. "Just get well and come home."

Carl did not get well. His leg became infected. The infection spread. It was a month before it could be confirmed. Carl would never walk again. He was wheelchair-bound, unable to farm, unable to dance, unable even to tap his toes with the music.

"I couldn't see him. I wrote him this awful letter instead."

In the letter, she tried to explain that she cherished his friendship but said they were never meant to be together. She lied. She didn't know where the words came from. She sobbed as she wrote, heard a voice in her head saying, Coward. Still, she wrote, and then she signed and sealed the envelope and ran to the mailbox to post it, shoving the letter into the slot so hard, she sliced her knuckle open. She remembers sucking the blood, how it tasted of iron. She remembers gorging on dinner that night, ham and macaroni, the sweet maple crunch of ham rind between her teeth, the salty mush of macaroni in her throat. Sweet tea with lemon chunks. Dense vanilla cake with brown-sugar icing crawling down the sides.

•

Six months after, many of the Hancock County boys got leave. The day before the men were to return to the valley, Edna got a call from Erla Thornberry.

"Let me talk to Jean."

Aneita Jean picked up the phone and could feel the hostility on the other end like a sunburn.

"I hear you got a ring," Erla snapped.

"Yes." She had received several, actually.

"You better not hurt Don," Erla hissed over the phone.
Aneita Jean said nothing.

"You hear me? You better not hurt my son."

•

The next afternoon, Erla pulled up at Phoenix Avenue
with Don beside her. The car hadn't stopped before he
leapt out and ran to the door. When Aneita Jean answered,
Don fell to his knees and hugged her waist.

"My beautiful Jeannie," he said, smiling, gripping
tighter. Erla went inside, looking Aneita Jean in the eye as
she passed. They stood like that until Aneita Jean couldn't
stomach it another second and suggested they go for a drive.

Cruising through the woods, she watched Don drive,
his sinewy forearms pulsing as he turned the wheel. She
traced the angles of his profile, the tufts of his black hair,
which was trying like hell to curl, even though it had been
buzz-cut to military length. She noted the way his knees
poked slightly through the fabric of his pants, how his belt
buckled just to the right of his zipper. His fingernails were
clean, his skin scrubbed white, even his ears, which stuck
out slightly, but nothing like Orville's. His sleeves were
rolled high, well above his elbow, and they strained, as
always, around his biceps.

"What are you gawking at?" he asked, jerking his head
to look at her, then laughing. He seemed giddy, drunk from
the motion of the car undulating over hill and dale, from
the gaze of the woman he loved. He was handsome. A serious man, made lighter by her.

They parked the car in the holler and he reached for her.

"They're sending me to Missouri day after tomorrow," he said, holding her hand gently, as if he feared it might break. She looked down at her hand in his, and as his long fingers wrapped around hers, she said, "I think I'll go with you."

It wasn't a decision, but an instinct.

"What?"

"I. Think. I'll. Go. With. You."

And with that, he fell into her, clutching her again as he had on the porch, and she could hear him breathing fast. She knew instantly what she had done, what she had chosen. She knew she would always be loved. And she hugged him back, wondering if he could feel her heart.

•

D onald Leslie Thornberry and Aneita Jean Blair were married on August 21, 1944. On her wedding day, Grandmother "didn't do much but polish my nails and put up the top of my hair. I had an appointment at the beauty parlor but canceled it because Don liked my hair as natural as possible." She borrowed a hankie from Sara Hocking and inserted a dime from the neighbors in her shoe for luck.

The ceremony was fast and simple. "But boy did Don's hands shake."

The notice in the newspaper read:

Chester Social Notes—Miss Aneita Jean Blair, daughter of Mr. and Mrs. A. C. Blair, Phoenix Ave., became the bride of Sgt. Donald Leslie Thornberry, son of Mr. and Mrs. Alvin H. Thornberry, Grant

St., Newell, at a ceremony performed Friday night
at 7 o'clock in the parsonage of the Newell Presbyterian Church. The bride, who is a graduate of
Chester High School in 1938 and was employed at
the National Church Supply Co., was gowned in
aqua blue with white accessories. Her shoulder cor-
sage was yellow rosebuds and gardenias. She also
wore a string of pearls, the gift of her parents.

Erla had taken my grandmother to Pittsburgh to buy the
dress. It had buttons down the front and flowers sewn on the
neck and sleeve. Her shoes were white and had ankle straps.
She also bought the ring. The only folks at the service were
Don's sister Velma and her husband, Paul. At the reception,
they served grape punch and tuna sandwiches. In a list
shoved in the memory book, Grandmother writes, "I didn't
have much of a trousseau but here's what I brought along on
my honeymoon: Purple suit and beanie to match, black suit,
navy suit, brown silk jersey dress, pleated, gray chalk-striped
suit and gray tam for traveling, navy slacks, three shirts,
three shorts, black chesterfield, blue chesterfield, other
dresses and skirts and blouses too numerous to mention."

On a shorter list she records her wedding gifts. Aunt
Mae, pillow slips. Dad, hand-painted ashtray with our
names on it. Mom, $25 grill waffle iron. Brother Al, snazzy
cigarette lighter. Mrs. Thornberry, luncheon set. National
Church, picture of the Ohio River painted by Cyril T.

The next day, after a furious bout of packing, she and
Don climbed in Erla's car and headed to Camp Crowder in
Joplin, Missouri, where Don was stationed. As she turned
to wave good-bye, Aneita Jean saw her father weeping in
the yard beside his prize peonies.

•

Velma and Erla accompanied the couple to Missouri. "I want to see you settle someplace right," Erla said by way of explanation.

Their first night as man and wife, Erla, Velma, Don, and Aneita Jean slept in a tourist camp outside Joplin. Since they could only afford one room, Velma turned the radio up loud.

•

In the years that followed, my grandmother often revisited that day she and Don took a drive in the holler. It amused and frightened her how abruptly her life changed. How decisions can be like car accidents, sudden and full of consequence.

"I married him because I knew he loved me the most."

The day my grandmother decided to marry Don Thornberry was also the day she realized that she would never leave Hancock County.

"He was a Newellie," she says. "He wasn't going anywhere."

She remembers how they rode home that day in a calm quiet. And she remembers how, for the first time in her entire life, she felt relaxed. She wasn't going anywhere.

"Drive slower, drive slower," she whispered to Don. And he did, the two of them creeping along the woods' edge, the crunch of leaves audible beneath the tires.

"I sure do love you, Jean," he said.

"I know you do," she answered.

•

When they got engaged, Don was not thinking about the particulars, about the everlasting grind of marriage, the details of which he could scarcely imagine. He did not, for example, imagine his wife hiding shopping packages under the bed (filmy dresses bought with kitchen money and donned only in secret in the bathroom to make her feel, just for a second, as exquisite as she had once been), or imagine himself hiding his overflowing ashtray under the coffee table (once she quit smoking and demanded he do the same). He did not envision the times he would want her to "just shut up," or the times he would hope as he drove that maybe if he was really lucky, the next car would slam head-on into his, sparing him another dinner across from a woman who wished with every cell of her being that she had married higher up the social ladder and never ceased to let him know it by sniffing at the stale bread and picking at the bubbles in the china and exhaling with the force of a gale wind. He did not consider her need, or the onus he would bear to shore up her fading beauty, to contradict what she herself saw to be true, and how once offered—"Jean, you look the same to me"—he'd be punished for his compliments because she felt them to be lies—"So I'm stupid as well as old?"

No, all he thought about was how beautiful she was then, at that moment, and how his head scraped the sky when she walked by his side, and how, beyond all his expectations, she had volunteered to walk there forever.

at H.t. Connor Hotel Rendezvous   Joplin Sept. 1945

The first time we had seen Ernie for 4 years.

CHAPTER SIXTEEN

Almost exactly one year after Don and Aneita Jean married, the war ended.

THANK GOD IT'S ALL OVER, ran the Tuesday, August 14, 1945, newspaper headline. In a related story, the *East Liverpool Review* reported, "Work to resume tomorrow," stressing that all potteries would recommence normal business as soon as the celebration was over.

"We knew the war had ended because there was screaming in the streets," says Grandmother. "We were all so glad to be going home."

In the valley, hundreds of potters lined the walkways to view the victory parade led by fifteen mounted horses. The horses were trailed by the Chester High School Band, the

Purple and Gold Band Mothers, the Chester Volunteer Fire-
men, the Newell Drum and Bugle Corps, the military police
of the Chester Civilian Defense Council, and a fleet of decorated bicycles. Songs were played from a truck-mounted
PA system and the whole march concluded with a free
dance party in the City Hall auditorium.

Don and Jean left Joplin, Missouri, and met up with
Don's brother, Ernie, on the way home.

In the photograph of the reunion, the three of them are
seated at a circular table in the Hotel Connor's dining
room. There are seven cocktail tumblers and three shot
glasses on the table. All three of them are holding lighted
cigarettes between their fingers. Don and Ernie are in army
uniform. Aneita Jean wears a white shirt and black jacket, a
broach (from Cyril) at her throat. She looks tired. Don
looks pleased, a half smile on his face. Ernie looks angry
and drunk and leans heavy into the glass table, his elbow
nudging his brother's arm. It was the first time they had
seen each other in four years.

"Don and his no-good drunk-ass brother," Grandmother says every time she sees the picture.

•

Back in Newell, they learned that forty-three boys from
Hancock County had been killed or wounded, including W. E. Wells, Jr. Alan and Forbes had survived. When she
pulled up to Phoenix Avenue, her brothers were waiting on
the porch. They all hugged, but something had changed.
Forbes seemed embarrassed to be home, and he left for
Washington shortly after, where he married a stunning

debutante who found his hardscrabble background colorful and exciting, not that he spoke of it much.

Alan and Nancy also left, he for the West Coast and she
for university study. It was as if they couldn't stand to be in
the valley anymore—there were too many shadows. Aneita
Jean packed them off with the college savings she no longer
needed, and when Alan became a respected teacher and
Nancy a successful painter, she felt their successes as if they
were hers.

Andrew Blair was still depressed, having never recovered from Petey's death. When his surviving sons went on
to live full lives and accomplish much, he remained unre-
sponsive, swallowed up by the lost potential of the boy he
loved best. After the war, he quit his position at the pottery
and retreated to his studio for good.

Edna was sicker than ever. My grandmother remembers
the day she came home, watching her mother descend the
stairs one at a time, her hands gripping the railing till they
whitened at the knuckles.

"It was the first time I had seen her so bad. My heart
just fell."

So she moved in. My grandmother and Don unloaded
their bags at Phoenix Avenue and stayed for three years,
cooking, cleaning, and working at the pottery to pay the
bills.

HLC had taken a hit with the war, losing many workers, but, as always, the company found ways to persevere.
Women did the men's work. Technology improved, and
with it came a need for fewer bodies in the plants. After the
war, the boycotts on foreign pottery ended and HLC found
itself groping for business. Japanese potters were paid less

than their American counterparts, and the factories they labored in were sleeker and predictably efficient. Layoffs began. It would seem to many as if they never stopped. Eventually, Knowles China liquidated, laying off five hundred potters. HLC would be forced to let 2,800 workers go. Where more than fifty-five potteries had once flourished, only two remained, Hall in East Liverpool and the unsinkable HLC in Newell.

With so many men out of work, Don began to worry about his job, a fear he kept from his wife, who never needed something else to worry about. As it was, she was consumed.

"I thought my mother would be so pleased that we had moved in," says Grandmother. "I was wrong. She asked us to leave. I think it made her sick to have me there."

"You're in my way," Edna would say, trying to flush her daughter out of the kitchen. "For God's sake, get out."

"I knew she wasn't well, but I didn't know she was dying," Grandmother says. "So we left."

The day before Edna died, Aneita Jean got a call from the neighbors while she was playing gin rummy.

"Your mother is feeling poorly," they said.

"So I rush over to Phoenix Avenue and I get this 'I'm fine.' We tried to take her to the hospital, but she refused to go. She was stubborn like that. So we prayed for her. Fine lot of good that did."

The next afternoon, Aneita Jean went home, to discover Edna had called the East Liverpool hospital herself that morning, told them, "Come get me," and died alone on a gurney just after lunchtime.

Though Edna Blair had never been a potter, and though she had rarely left her house, her obituary in the *East Liver-*

pool Review ran five inches, longer than the local pharma-
cist's and only slightly shorter than the tavern owner's.

"She was always the warmest person," remembers
Grandmother. "Nothing like me at all."

•

Andrew Blair would survive his wife for another thirteen
years. In his solitude, he let his studio disintegrate.
It became crowded, filled with exhibit jars holding two-
headed pigs, with papers and stacked plates, all sodden and
musty, and with bottles holding liquid gold, clotted paint-
brushes sticking out the tops. The squatty decorating kiln
was crumbling, and Andrew bolstered it with a stack of
stones, different-colored boulders he painted with castle
spikes. There was one bare hanging lightbulb, which swung
and swathed everything—the chaotic, reeling shelves, the
crates packed with shredded paper, the lurching towers of
ware—in a discordant glare. Outside, the studio looked as
if a healthy breeze could knock it flat. Inside, the place
stank of newborn kittens.

Neighborhood children were afraid of Andrew. Because
he did not smile. Because he was so strange compared to his
wife, who had always proffered a hen-shaped candy dish
overflowing with Hershey's Kisses. And who, when they
came for dinner, set up a table on the porch and served leg
of lamb with fried mint, while weird old man Blair would
hide in his studio, looking out through the cracking wood
at his gazing ball, his tulips and peonies unnaturally bright
and bent in the reflection.

For thirteen years, Andrew lived at Phoenix Avenue by
himself, with the exception of Annie, a black woman my

grandmother hired to check on him once a week. Against all probability, Annie and Andrew Blair got on. They got on so well that when Annie had a baby boy, she named him Blair, a tribute that touched Andrew more than he expected. He died in his sleep at a convalescent center when he was ninety-three years old. It was Annie who closed his eyes.

CHAPTER SEVENTEEN

In the memory book, there are no photographs after 1945. It ends with a picture of my grandmother perched on yet another Ford chrome bumper, smirking.

She wears a blouse, pencil skirt, saddle shoes with dark socks, thrice folded, and a plaid coat draped over her shoulders. Her hands are balled into fists and placed awkwardly in her lap. Her wild hair is harnessed in a discrete bow. It is impossible to know who took the photograph, but it could have been any one of a hundred men. That Aneita Jean Blair was now Mrs. Jean Thornberry was little deterrent.

Men kept calling. Now that it was forbidden, their attention was all the more thrilling. My grandmother never cheated on her husband per se, but the boundaries were awfully elastic.

After the Thornberrys evacuated Phoenix Avenue in 1947, they moved into a tiny shack across the alley from Erla Thornberry's house.

"Don's mother saw to it that we lived in that house," my grandmother says, sighing. "And I saw to it that we lived in a different one as soon as we could manage."

They settled at 415 Grant Street, three houses down from Erla and Alvin's, in a white two-story company house with four bedrooms and a stall bath. There was no laundry, so my grandmother was forced to do the wash every week at her mother-in-law's, a chore she dreaded like a leaching wound. Erla wanted something better for her son than the pottery. She also wanted something better for him than Aneita Jean Blair, and having failed on the second count, she doubled her resolve to succeed on the first.

"Don needs to quit the pottery, else he'll end up like his pappy."

"Yes, ma'am."

"Potters are low-rent, low-class good-for-nothings."

"Uh-huh."

"And I think more of my son than that, don't you?"

"Of course."

"So I suggest you tell Don to do something else before

it's too late. Boy won't listen to me anymore. Thinks he's all grown-up now."

"Well . . ."

"Be grown-up when he has some kids of his own. See how he likes it."

They found out soon enough, for on February 23, 1947, Don and Jean had a daughter, Jennifer Lynn Thornberry.

Jennifer Lynn was as lovely as a baby can be, a head full of hair, pink and plump as a piglet. She had her father's dark eyes and her mother's childhood scowl. Jean took one look at her and saw the future she'd never had.

After the baby, Don saved, and once they had three hundred dollars, he opened a walk-in grocery in a two-room shed near the pottery. He stocked it with fruit and salami, hard rolls and colas. Friends he played bridge with, Mr. and Mrs. Broomhall, took a great interest in the shop and encouraged Don.

Ever the hard worker, Don excelled at the grocery business. In a matter of months, he outgrew the shed and was able to purchase a brick building across from the post office. He taught himself to butcher and select produce. He brought in cuts of meat he knew the potters wanted, and he sold plenty. The store grew, eventually offering not just groceries but also a soda fountain and ice cream.

Don left for work every morning at seven o'clock in his apron and came home at noon for lunch. Jean would make him bologna sandwiches with butter and they would eat them together on the orange-yellow table in their tiny kitchen.

Afterward, Don would walk back to the store, staying until six o'clock, when he would return home for dinner, usually hamburgers and cucumber or pot roast and potato, with vanilla ice cream for dessert. After dinner, they would smoke on the porch and Don would tell his wife and daughter stories about elephants and monkeys, and Jean would close her eyes and pretend to be someplace else.

In 1949, baby Jenny was joined by Jody Jean. Two years later, Jill Leslie arrived. Jean Thornberry loved being pregnant, being bathed in concern and sympathy, being helped down the stoop, having groceries carried, lying down with impunity, being cosseted and coddled and cared for. She was radiant when she was with child. All three deliveries went off without a hitch and, thanks to the sleeping gas that was administered at the time, without her conscious knowledge.

When she awoke as a mother, as the caretaker—well, that was always something of a shock. She handled the children's infancies well enough, but once the girls became toddlers, the incessant whining and need drove Jean to fits.

Here is what my mother, Jennifer, remembers about her youth. She remembers her mother draped on the sofa, sick or tired, or both. She remembers her mother circling the upstairs hallway, wailing at all hours of the night. She remembers her mother balanced on the trembling knees of her and her sister's dates, picking at their hair and running her manicured index finger over their flushed cheeks.

She remembers that, and the scenes. There were always scenes. Like the time she was five minutes late coming home from a date and Jean was up, waiting, her silhouette in the window, rocking. When Jenny opened the door, Jean nearly collapsed. She buckled over, sobbing and screaming.

"How could you do this to me? I was sick to death with worry."

All the noise brought Don downstairs, and when Jenny turned to him as the voice of reason, he shook his head fiercely.

"Don't you talk back to your mother" was all he said.

"She wasn't constitutionally equipped for the job," says Jennifer.

"My nerves, you know," says Grandmother.

•

It was Don who taught his three girls how to clean, iron, cook, and dress themselves. It was Don who showed them how to plant seeds and jump rope and count change. It was Don who checked their spelling and laid out their Girls' Club uniforms and made sure they practiced their French. Don was the mother and the father, and the arrangement was what it had to be, because Jean Thornberry was a lot of things, but the perfect fifties housewife was not one of them.

She did impart some lessons.

In a photograph from my mother's memory book, she and her sisters are standing in front of Jean, who has her arms weakly draped around the three of them. Eight-year-old Jody is wearing a pink ruffled dress with a ribbon and flower appliqués across the chest. Six-year-old Jill is in a floral-print dress with puffy sleeves and a blue satin ribbon belt. Ten-year-old Jennifer, flanked by her siblings, is in a similar pink floral-print dress with a pink ribbon belt and scalloped collar. Each girl's hair is combed into place and fastened with yet more ribbon. They are all perfect dreamy confections of girlhood, except that none of them is smiling. Their expressions are heavy, reflecting a skepticism and wariness incongruous with the faces of little girls in Easter frocks.

If it even was Easter. Jean dressed her girls in formal wear whenever the mood struck. She clipped their hair and yanked three pairs of white gloves over their tiny hands. She pinned on pillbox hats and bonnets, then stood them all up in front of her for photographs, much as her father had done twenty years earlier in the West Virginia holler, when the world was starving and Petey Dink was still alive and the idea of babies was something my grandmother knew only from picture books.

"My beautiful girls," she'd say.

•

When she was fifteen, Jennifer Lynn Thornberry was chosen queen of the Thermo-Jacs in the country store contest. When she was sixteen, she was voted Miss Leap Year. She was also in every prom court from freshman year to graduation, an honor that had her riding around the football field in an open convertible, wearing a gown and heels, her gloved hand waving softly to the crowd.

"She was never voted the queen," says Grandmother. "Those other girls were just jealous, you know."

At fourteen, Jody Jean Thornberry became head cheerleader of Wells High. She also started eating her dinners in the living room by herself, because she decided that Newell was a hellhole and she wanted nothing to do with anyone who chose to live there.

Jill, a six-foot-two blonde who looked like Petey Dink's

twin, was told she had modeling potential when she was just thirteen, but ultimately she declined to pursue that line of work, as it didn't involve horses or dogs or kitties.

As all three girls grew into puberty, the number of boys passing through 415 Grant Street was staggering. Jennifer dated at least three boys each weekend night. Jody preferred to go steady, for about two weeks. Jill liked animals better than men, but it didn't stop boys from dropping by, nor did it keep her from getting pregnant at age nineteen by a handsome Pole who was almost seven feet tall.

When the girls were still in high school, Jean started seeing a chiropractor for her migraines. Don loaded up the car with his girls and took the family to the doctor's office in Pennsylvania, an hour's drive.

"We'd have to wait in the car while she went in there and did whatever it was she was doing," says Jennifer. "What a chiropractor had to do with headaches, I've yet to figure out."

Along with the chiropractor, Jean began consulting a psychic, who told her, "Your feelings are very intense. You can be oversolicitous. You find peace in things of beauty. You are likely to seek new freedom and excitement through your relationships, especially those of the opposite sex."

"Some psychic," said Jody.

•

In time, Ernie joined his brother, Don, at the store. They named the place Thornberry Brothers Grocery and hung a plastic sign above the front door. It didn't take long before Ernie made an ass of himself in front of customers, unable to locate the canned peas, too drunk to count bills. He became a burden, but Don kept him on, knowing he had no place else to go.

The Broomhalls, in an act of treachery, started another grocery down the block to compete with Thornberry Brothers. The opening started a turf war between the former friends, who were now competing for pottery business. Broomhall spread rumors at HLC that Don's meat was rotten. Don threatened to beat the living crap out of Broomhall if he kept on lying about his store. Broomhall retaliated by getting Ernie drunk and milking him of all of Don's hamburg secrets. Don adjusted his recipe, adding more fat. Broomhall got a beer license. Don asked the Reverend Haddock if he should get a beer license. The Reverend Haddock said absolutely not, that liquor was sinful. The Broomhalls' business quadrupled. Don's waned. The Reverend Haddock shopped at Broomhall's, unbothered by the sinful bottles stocked next to the iced tea and Pepsi.

"Broomhall went to the same church as we did, and the preacher would get up and say, 'Mr. Broomhall furnished the ham for today's supper. Shop at Broomhall's.' And meanwhile, Don had furnished paint and refinished all the pews, but the preacher never mentioned it because Don didn't slip him free liquor."

"Son of a bitch Reverend Haddock," she says, still fuming fifty years later. "Fish Haddock, I called him. Son of a bitch."

Broomhall was eventually hauled in for tax fraud. The Reverend Haddock asked that everyone pray for his forgiveness, which prompted the Thornberrys to stop with the church thing altogether.

Broomhalls or not, Don was no businessman. He was

too soft. When the potteries started laying people off, he operated on credit, never collecting payment, just adding up the charges on a long, yellowing list that was pinned to a beam behind the cash register. Sometimes he skipped the formality and just gave away the groceries for free. He kept entire families fed for years, delivering the milk and bread himself, never speaking of it, and as my grandmother astutely notes, "You can't make money that way."

And he didn't. He just kept doing the right thing, being Sir Don, helping his brother, who robbed him; feeding the mouths that never thanked him; giving out lollipops and comic books; and, when his house got small with the noise of new life, being the father and the mother to three girls, seeing that they grew healthy and strong. And then, just when he thought the wind was at his back, his wife checked reason at the door, and Sir Don inherited a whole new set of problems.

As a child, my grandmother was crazy in the same way that all women are who are born in a town too small for their wild fever, a town that scrapes them on the edges and tries to sand off the sharpness. She was the kind of crazy that comes from being aware of the insanity around you. As an adult, my grandmother became a different sort of crazy, the kind that comes from damaged genes and a head full of too much. The kind where you unhinge and even the dog watches you carefully.

In 1955, after a month of watching Jean pace the hallway all night weeping, Don made her an appointment with Dr. Brand.

Jean told the doctor that she was worried. That she didn't know anything but the inside of her house. That she would watch Don with her young girls and wonder how he could be so patient, so calm, when all she wanted to do was toss them out the window of a moving car.

Dr. Brand prescribed some blue pills and told Don to take her out every weekend, unless he wanted her to end up in the bin.

Jean took the pills, then learned to take others. By the time she was eighty, she would swallow ten pills a day—antidepressants, two types of steroids to help her breathe, heart medication, migraine medications, painkillers, blood pressure medication, antianxiety pills.

With Dr. Brand's pills came fresh boredom and an unwelcome coherence. Everything became clear. She was living in a town she loathed, a mother, but only a mother, not a singer, or a painter, or anything that anyone would ever talk about. She was aging, her breasts shot from nursing, her skin loose under her arms and knees. She remembered something her mother, Edna, had told her in a rare moment of brutality.

"Don't get used to those men looking at you every time you come in the room, because it won't last."

It seemed impossible at the time. And yet, as the years passed, and her daughters grew lovelier, and the boys who called no longer blushed for her, she was forced to consider the grim truth that the only thing she had ever counted on was leaving her.

This realization did two things to my grandmother: It made her nastier, and it made her funnier. They were symbiotic inclinations.

When her girls brought home sincere, solid men, Jean would suck her teeth.

"Don't you like him, Mom?"

"What's not to like?"

Don got the worst of it. When she turned thirty-five, she began to tear him down, to pick at him. She slammed him and defiled him, mocked him and wallowed in his ugly parts, until her skin crawled at the thought of his hand on hers.

"Be quiet, Jean!" he would scream, his face red with confusion. "Be quiet!"

He wasn't the one.

He wasn't the one, she thought.

But oh, how he loved her.

It wasn't all bad. There was Christmas, with tinsel bunting, cakes shaped like clowns; muskie-fishing trips to Canada; a tidy house; food on the table. Jean and Don danced every Saturday at the Elks' lodge in Weirton, just like the doctor had ordered. Don, slim and tall in his best suit. Jean, lean and soaring in a flowy dress. He would spin and dip her with ease; she would twirl and yield with confidence. It was a gorgeous ballet to watch. It was like everyone said: They fit together perfectly.

•

I saw them dance one summer when I was visiting. It was 1978. Their girls had long since become women and moved away. Jody married a Pittsburgh footballer and moved with him to Buffalo, where he played for the Bills. Jill was raising her son alone and studying for her master's degree in psychology. Jennifer, my mother, had already earned her degree in psychology and was setting up a practice in Jacksonville, helping the children of emotionally abusive parents.

I was ten and already gawky. Tall, with thick calves, I

hunted frogs in the sewer, played soccer on the boys' team, and did my best to forget I was a girl at all.

The summer I was visiting, Grandmother introduced me to Warna Kay, a thirteen-year-old who lived just up the block, right next to HLC. Warna was all girl, a brunette, who had wings cut into her hair, and breasts already, and a bottomless tan that she earned by lathering herself with Crisco and sitting in the yard, wearing nothing but cutoffs and a bandanna for a top.

"Very creative," I said of her fashion choice.

"What's that mean?" she asked, chewing on a grass stem.

That night after we watched *The Lawrence Welk Show,* I told my grandmother how Warna Kay was so stupid, she didn't even know what *creative* meant, and my grandmother looked me in the eye and said, "Great gifts come with great responsibilities," and though I didn't really understand what she meant, shame churned in my belly.

Later, between dances at the Elks' lodge, I saw Grandmother talking with many women whose husbands seemed more interested in her than in their wives. I saw her whisper in the wives' ears and saw them laugh and slap their knees and nod knowingly. It was as if they had been girlhood pals, friends all their lives, but of course they hadn't.

•

Although there are no photographs in the memory book after 1945, there are clippings. Newspaper reports of Forbie's ascension in the Republican party, Alan's teaching awards and military certificates, birthday greetings from Nancy, telegrams from old beaux, the occasional card.

"Jeannie, you are coy, witty, quick with repartee, intelligent and acquainted with the arts. You are easy to love. I do love you. Keep in this world, dear. It needs people like you. Your fan, No. 72007."

There are only three letters shoved amid the clutter. One was from me. I must have been about eleven years old.

Dear Grandmother, I am very sorry I haven't written in so long, but I have been busy. How is the store going? Good I hope. My dad keeps saying you should get Beefalo. He says it would really boost your business. Ha! I got your pictures, the ones where you were modeling in the sexy gown, and they were great! You are very pretty. I have a new boyfriend now. His name is Ivy Smith. He is really nice and he always says nice things about people. I know you would like him. Only one problem, I don't know if he likes me.

The second letter was written by my grandfather in 1994. Scribbled in pencil on lined stationery, it is barely legible. Grandmother saved it as proof. She needed something to show the doctors. It says, in part:

I wanted to be someone. Paper boy. Take away garbage for 20 cents. Always looking for a way to make money. Then after the war I decided to go into business. I started a small grocery for the people in Newell, West Virginia. And some things were a snap. Bags of beans. Everything they liked. All kinds of bananas. Oranges. Carrots. They all had trouble. I bought what they wanted. Potatoes. Celery. Watermelons. Apples. Onions. And Strawberries. And some lettuce. Almost everything.

The letter continues for seven pages, front and back. With each page, it gets more incoherent, a list of grocery items, interrupted by tirades against the government and pitiful pleas for recognition. A paper clipped at the end is the third letter, this one from Jean, dated March 20.

Darling Don: I got ready to come to see you but I couldn't make it. Please don't be mad at me sweetheart. I really can't help it. I'll keep trying hard to get better. You know I want to come. The weather will get better soon and you'll be able to go outside. I want the nurse to bring home your big picture in uniform. I don't want it to get lost. With love, XXX, Jean.

•

It wasn't all bad. There were gin games on the porch, walks in the holler, Easter ham, piano lessons, fireflies caught in mason jars, pottery picnics with fried chicken and biscuits and gravy. But there was also his unexpected madness, her growing hysteria, and the loneliness that descends on a house full of fear and empty of children and reason.

"After I married Don, I became a hoopie because I moved below the Newell Bridge. I remember one time, before we married, we went on a date and he was wearing his father's pants, and he ran around the corner and fell, and they ripped. He was horrified. I tried to get him to laugh it off. I just wanted to make him feel better. I always wanted him to feel better."

•

Donald Thornberry died in February of 1997. He had lived his last five years in a nursing home for Alzheimer's patients. Grandmother remembers the first day she dropped him off and how he wailed and grabbed her arms.

"I can't live without my Jeannie," he cried, screaming as the orderlies tugged him through the swinging doors. Grandmother stood there, her eyes fixed on the dark space between the doors, watching as it grew smaller and smaller, the doors swishing noisily, until it finally became a thin black line.

When Grandfather died, he was willow-thin and sunken in like a fallen cake. The Alzheimer's made him forget to eat. So he withered.

Grandmother visited him every Sunday, staring into his drawn face. In time, he no longer remembered her name, but she visited anyway, and made sure to look nice when she did.

Then she stopped going. Wrote that letter. Decided she could not watch her husband die.

When he finally passed away, it was because the family had decided he should stop being force-fed and pilled like a dog. The time for cringing was over. They tell us he went quietly, breath bleeding into the air, then nothing.

The funeral was held in Charlotte, and Grandmother

wore a creamy white dress and matching pumps. "Black," she explained, "is not my color."

Grandfather had been made up with rouge and powder and dressed in a suit for the viewing.

"He looks good, don't you think?" Grandmother asked no one in particular. She patted his cheek, said, "I love you." Kissed him hard on his painted lips. Said, "Good-bye, Daddy Don."

At the reception, grandmother danced with somebody else's husband. She was winded—it's hard to dance in your late seventies—but she smiled through her discomfort, fanned herself with her palm.

"You are a fine dancer," she cooed to her partner. "You're making me dizzy." The man grinned, straightened his back.

"Don't you think we ought to sit down?" Jean suggested. "Or should we continue down the path to trouble?" She raised her eyebrows, tilted her head.

"I'm crazy, you know," she said, laughing, her fingers gripping his shoulder even tighter. She looked over his shoulder at his wife and winked.

After the funeral, the family took photos. We stacked up in front on the azalea bushes, shoulder-to-shoulder, all of us stained and puffed from crying. Grandmother propped herself in front, at the center of the pack.

"Smile with your eyes," she commanded through her teeth.

And though we all felt ridiculous, we did.

Me at Schiff. Park

I look terrible huh?

CHAPTER EIGHTEEN

At her eightieth birthday party, my grandmother sits at the head of the long banquet table in the Crab Shack bar. The family has rented out the room, and all of us are there, minus Uncle Glen of the bad balls. Grandmother is glowing in a canary yellow twin set and color-coordinated linen pants. On her feet are ballet flats.

The tabletop is littered with cocktails and half-eaten

shrimp trays. We get drunk and stuff ourselves as we wait, one by one, to have our moment with Grandmother. When it's our turn, we walk to the table head, then squat down to tell her about our lives, our children, our memories of her. When it's my turn, I show her a photograph of my newborn daughter, Dixie Jean, named after her.

"She's beautiful," says Grandmother. "Everything that comes from me is beautiful."

Twelve months later, my grandmother is strapped in a nursing home wheelchair, towing an oxygen tank behind her. She has suffered a stroke. The stroke has snatched away her voice. She can still talk, but it is difficult. She cannot sing. Her doctors say she suffers from "dementia and an inability to distinguish real from unreal," a diagnosis that makes her daughters chuckle.

"If that's from the stroke," says Jody, "she had one a long time ago."

Her youngest daughter, Jill, lives nearby, and Jill's son Scott brings his girlfriend to make up Grandmother's face and tease and style her hair once a week. She wears it in a fashionable bob, no bangs. The makeup is the same, but now it looks a little freakish, the orange rouge and lipstick sliding into the deep wrinkles and the hollows of her cheeks.

I look at her crazy slip-slidey face and suddenly I am fourteen again, a gangly five foot nine, in junior high school, invisible. I am busying myself on the bus, listening to Van Halen on my Walkman, while the petite girls, the adorable, tiny girls, get groped in the backseats.

"What's wrong?" my grandmother asked me that summer when I slunk off the plane.

"Nothing," I muttered.

That night, Grandmother dressed me in one of her old ball gowns. It had layers of chiffon bustled up under a shell of purple satin. She sat me barefoot on the bed and took my picture.

"Aren't you something," she said, adjusting the chiffon over my knobby knees. "You in a gown and your hoopie shoes."

I sulked, scratched my bare ankle.

"Something ugly," I whispered.

Grandmother put the camera down and stood in front of me.

"You," she said, her hand holding my chin, "couldn't be ugly if you tried." Her voice was firm and direct, without a trace of pity, as if she were simply reciting a fact. Tallahassee is the capital of Florida. You couldn't be ugly if you tried.

•

My grandmother has mellowed. "When you get older, you like everybody more. You get some sense."

Before the stroke, there were more jokes. The family would visit and she would crack faces. When we left, she'd sing.

"Ev'ry time we say goodbye, I die a little." Nursing home humor. Funny stuff.

When she receives visitors now, Grandmother leans forward as best she can. If you hug her, she will stay there, tilted into her wheelchair bar, her head in your neck, for as long as you can bear it. Her skin is papery and tears easily. Her weight has dropped well below one hundred pounds. And still, when she pulls back, when she rights herself and eyes you, who are hunched and guilty and torturing yourself with anticipated grief, she manages a small nod.

"You look very nice," she says. "How about me?"

EPILOGUE

I have not been in West Virginia for too long now. The last time I visited, it smelled the same, but the view had worsened. There was trash on the highway, and burned-out cars in the holler. The Victorian parks and trolley lines were long gone. The buildings and shops were still there, but many had been condemned, the windows cracked and jammed with old newspapers. The HLC zoo was empty, but rumor had it that the monkeys still lived in the holler, and that if you listened, you could hear them crashing plates to the ground, the scream of breaking china echoing off the riverbank walls.

I walked down Phoenix Avenue, past my grandmother's childhood home, only to find it had been boarded up. Someone bought it, then was laid off, or ran out of money, and so it's the bank's house now, which is to say that it's been left to rot, like everything else in the town. Andrew Blair's studio was still standing. Stained mattresses blocked the doors and windows from the inside, but the hardware from his lunch bell was still hanging, rusty and quiet, and his name was still carved on the doorjamb, "A. C. Blair," the letters black with age.

I thought, This is not how it was. I wanted it to be beautiful. I wanted it to rise from beneath the belly like a flock of birds.

I thought, This is not how it was. Or maybe it was, but I am not who I was, because I am grown, no longer a dreamy child who falls asleep on hard chairs, in scorching cars, slick against the seats, making my own comfort by marrying myself to the world around me.

I thought, This is not how it was. Or maybe it was, but this time I am alone, my grandmother is not with me, there are no stories being told, no songs being sung. This time, the place is dead quiet, dead empty, just plain dead, as if my grandmother's leaving has taken all the music with her.

Oh, the West Virginia hills!
Where my girlhood's hours were passed;

Where I often wandered lonely,
And the future tried to cast;
Many are our visions bright
Which the future ne'er fulfills;
But how sunny were my day-dreams
In those West Virginia hills!

Country roads, take me home.

Ah shit-anya, piss-anya, lasagna.

Aneita Jean Blair Thornberry died March 19, 2002. The funeral was held in Charlotte, North Carolina, in the same chapel as her husband's service years earlier. The preacher was named Reverend Pigg. He spoke at a plywood lectern beside her baby blue casket. Inside, my grandmother wore a matching baby blue linen dress with a patterned silk scarf arranged around her reedy neck like a ruff. Her skin was sallow and caked with cheap beige makeup, but her outfit was sharp and would have complemented her eyes, had they been open.

Reverend Pigg spoke little about my grandmother, preoccupied as he was with being a salesman for God. He urged all of us to consider taking Jesus into our lives, especially those of us who had never done so before, which was about all of us in attendance. Reverend Pigg spoke at lightning speed about salvation and the peace of heaven while we, the godless lot, shifted in flimsy plastic chairs. When he urged us to remember the "special times we all shared with Grandmother and would share again in heaven if we came to Jesus," I laughed. My grandmother is not going to heaven, fool. I looked at the casket and imagined her chuckling inside it.

Ten minutes later, my grandmother was buried beside her husband in a tiny plot of rich southern soil with a negligible view of an apartment complex. Reverend Pigg gave it one last shot as her casket was lowered into the dirt— "Only Jesus can provide real comfort"—but by then we were all sobbing. Her three daughters were toppled into one another like bowling pins, and I was standing alone, as close as I could get to the edge.

Her obituary read, "Aneita Jean Thornberry, age 81, died Wednesday, March 19, 2002 in Presbyterian Wesley Care Center. Born September 30, 1920 in Chester, West Virginia she was a daughter of the late Andrew and Edna McHenry Blair. She was a homemaker and artist."

"I put that artist part in," said Jill, her baby. "It's what she always wanted to be."

•

Above ground, life goes on, even in West Virginia. Homer Laughlin is still up and running. Fiesta Ware has become a bona fide collectible. Hip kids and pottery fans from all over scour the earth for original pieces in mint condition, with no evidence of the long life they've led. The miniature green donkey now sells for $225.

"Who'da thunk it?" my grandmother would say. "A pig's ass is pork."

•

In my memory book, I have a picture of my grandmother. She is wading into a pearl white creek, her filmy dress lifted to her hips and scrunched into her hands. Her shoulders are rolled back. Her hair is a riot of curls. She has turned her face away from the lens. But anyone can tell that she was beautiful.

ACKNOWLEDGMENTS

This book would never have been possible without the generous cooperation of Homer Laughlin China, the residents of Newell and Chester, the Wells family, and the potters themselves, who graciously let me into their lives.

In addition, many books assisted in my research, most particularly *The History of Newell and Vicinity,* published by the Newell Bi-Centennial Book Commission; the West Virginia Heritage collection, compiled by the West Virginia Heritage Foundation; and *Homer Laughlin, A Giant Among Dishes* by Jo Cunningham. The staff of the East Liverpool Pottery Museum were also invaluable in their contributions.

I would also like to gratefully acknowledge the kindness and support of the following people: Gary Belsky for his energy; Alex Postman for her good judgment; Lisa Hendricksson for her insight; Susan Reed for her hand-holding; Arthur Cooper for giving me enough rope; Lucy Danziger for her enthusiasm; Melissa Chessher for her gorgeous spirit; Daniel Ferrara for his inspiration; Jordan Pavlin and Sonny Mehta for their patience and optimism; Sarah Chalfant for saying all the right things and working harder than anyone else I know; my husband, Nick, for being unflappable; and, lastly, my family for their bravery and pluck.

ABOUT THE AUTHOR

Allison Glock is thirty-three years old and lives in New Jersey with her family. This is her first book.

A NOTE ON THE TYPE

The text of this book was set in Sabon, a typeface designed by Jan Tschichold (1902–1974), the well-known German typographer. Based loosely on the original designs by Claude Garamond (c. 480–1561), Sabon is unique in that it was explicitly designed for hotmetal composition on both the Monotype and Linotype machines as well as for filmsetting. Designed in 1966 in Frankfurt, Sabon was named for the famous Lyons punch cutter Jacques Sabon, who is thought to have brought some of Garamond's matrices to Frankfurt.

Composed by North Market Street Graphics
Lancaster, Pennsylvania

Printed and bound by R. R. Donnelley and Sons
Harrisonburg, Virginia

Designed by Iris Weinstein